MAURITSHUIS

ROYAL CABINET OF PAINTINGS

MAURITSHUIS

Guide

Published by
the Friends of the
Mauritshuis Foundation,
The Hague

[1]

Johannes de Baen, 1633-1702
*Portrait of Johan Maurits (1604-1679),
Count of Nassau-Siegen, founder of
the Mauritshuis*, after 1660
Canvas, 157.2 x 114 cm
Inv. 5

MAURITSHUIS

The official name
of the Mauritshuis – Royal Cabinet of Paintings
Mauritshuis – does not specifically state that it is a museum,
nevertheless that is its essential function.
This guide offers readers a selection of the highlights in
the museum, providing them first with general background
information about the name Mauritshuis,
the designation 'royal' and the history
of the paintings collection.

❧

The Mauritshuis was named after Johan Maurits (1604-1679), Count of Nassau-Siegen [fig. 1]. When Johan Maurits was born at Dillenburg in 1604, the Low Countries were at war – a struggle for independence which lasted for 80 years. Like his grandfather Jan (Johan) the Elder (1535-1606) – brother of Willem of Orange (1533-1584) – and his father Jan VII (1561-1623), Johan Maurits was destined for a military career. In 1621, at an exceptionally early age he joined the Dutch army. In 1626 he was made captain and in 1629 he was actively involved in the capture of Den Bosch, which earned his second cousin Frederik Hendrik the name 'Subduer of Cities'. The main feat accomplished by Johan Maurits himself was the conquest of the fort at Schenkenschans near Elten in 1636.

At the other end of the world, in South America, the clash of arms was no less violent. Portugal was forced to stand by helplessly as the Dutch troops rapidly took possession of their colony Brazil.

[2]
Frans Post, *c.*1612-1680
Brazilian landscape, 1667
Panel, 50 x 69 cm
Inv. 706

[3]
Albert Eckhout, *c.*1610-*c.*1666
*Two Brazilian tortoises, c.*1640
Paper on panel, 30.5 x 51 cm
Inv. 957 (permanent loan from the
Friends of the Mauritshuis Foundation,
The Hague)

8

In 1636 the Board of 19 Directors of the West India Company (the 'Heren XIX') decided to appoint a governor-general who would be in charge of the conquered territory, and approached Johan Maurits, the successful young army officer, for the post. Initially, his term of office was to be five years and the salary offered him was more than generous. On 25 October 1636 the newly appointed 'governor, captain and Admiral-General' set sail for the West aboard the Zutphen.

In Brazil Johan Maurits put an end to the Portuguese invasions south of Pernambuco and started building a new capital, Mauritsstad. By 1641 it had already attracted 5 to 10,000 inhabitants. Under his regime business flourished: teams of slaves were imported from Africa and put to work on the sugar plantations, the produce of which was sold in Holland. In 1641-1642 near Mauritsstad the Palace of Vrijburg was built in the Classical style. This became the seat of the colonial government. Johan Maurits's enlightened rule was to last until 1644. He was not simply there to exploit the country for its resources, but took a serious interest in the indigenous people, and their plants and animals.

The retinue of 'Maurits the Brazilian' included scholars and artists who apparently shared their patron's enthusiasm. It included both the natural scientist Georg Markgraf (1610-1643), author of *Historiae Rerum Naturalium Braziliae* and Willem Piso (1611-1678), Johan Maurits's personal physician, who wrote *De Medicina Brasiliensi*. In 1648 these scholarly works were published together under the general title *Historia Naturalis Brasiliae* by Elzevier in Amsterdam. Of the six artists he took along with him, two are now widely known: Frans Post (c.1612-1680), whose Brazilian landscapes [fig. 2] have the naive charm of works by Henri Rousseau 'le Douanier' (1844-1910), and Albert Eckhout (c.1610-c.1666), whose unprejudiced, realistic pictures of the Brazilian people, and their flora and fauna have never lost their impact [fig. 3]. Eckhout refrained from indulging in artistic embellishments but painted and drew simply what he saw. His observations are still of great scientific value.

Brazilians occasionally remember Johan Maurits's governorship of the colony with fondness. However, dissatisfaction with the support he received from the Board of Directors (the 'Heren XIX'), caused him to resign in 1642. On 6 May 1644 he handed the government

9

[4]
Gerard van Honthorst, 1590-1656
*Portrait of Stadholder Frederik Hendrik
(1584-1647) and his wife Amalia of Solms
(1602-1675)*, 1637-1638
Canvas, 213 x 201.4 cm
Inv. 104

[5]
Jan van Call, 1689-after 1748
*The Square with the Huygenshuis (left)
and the Mauritshuis (right)*, c.1690
Pen and brush, 17.8 x 27.5 cm
The Hague, Gemeentearchief,
inv. kl. A 666

[6]
Attributed to Abraham Lutma,
active c.1650
Portrait of Jacob van Campen (1596-1657)
Engraving, 41.6 x 24.8 cm
From: Jacob Vennekool, *Afbeelding
van 't Stadt-huys van Amsterdam,*
Amsterdam 1661

over to the authority of the High Court, after which the West India Company managed to hold on against the Portuguese for another ten years. After a period of seven years in South America, Johan Maurits returned to The Hague in August 1644 and soon after moved into his residence which had been built during his absence. The directors of the West India Company scornfully referred to it as the 'maison du sucre', because they thought the founder had made far too large a profit in the sugar trade. 'The Brazilian' firmly denied this.

In the second quarter of the seventeenth century The Hague went through its own golden age. At the age of 17, Johan Maurits had witnessed a sudden flourishing of court life in The Hague. 'Winter King' Frederik V (1596-1632) of the Palatinate took up residence at Kneuterdijk Palace in 1621, where Frederik Hendrik (1584-1647) was to meet Amalia of Solms (1602-1675). After their marriage in 1625 the Stadholder and his wife [fig. 4] built up a cultural environment at the Binnenhof (Inner Court), equal to the best anywhere in the world. Frederik Hendrik became an important patron of architecture. In particular, he patronised the architects Jacob van Campen (1596-1657) and Pieter Post (1608-1669), Frans Post's brother. In and around the royal residence new buildings sprang up rapidly: Honselaarsdijk (around 1632), Huis ter Nieuburch (1633/38), Noordeinde Palace (after 1641) and Huis ten Bosch Palace (completed in 1652). Constantijn Huygens (1596-1687) was of crucial importance in the realisation of their designs. He was the Stadholder's secretary, a true humanist, an accomplished musician, poet and architect and took a lively interest in the visual arts [fig. p. 59].

In 1631 the audit office deduced to sell parts of the Binnenhof Gardens which were never used: the 'Kooltuin' (cabbage garden) and 'Akertuin' (oak garden). Thus, as a result of Frederik Hendrik's personal meditation Johan Maurits and Constantijn Huygens each acquired a splendid plot of land to build on in the centre of The Hague. They were to become neighbours. In 1637 Huygens's house was completed [fig. 5] and as Johan Maurits had already left for Brazil, the Stadholder's secretary kept an eye on the advance of Johan Maurits's house while he was abroad. A stately building was erected in the Dutch Classical style, based on a plan by Jacob van Campen [fig. 6] and Constantijn Huygens on the foundations of an earlier structure,

Pieter Post, 1608-1669
Cross-section of the Mauritshuis, 1652
Pen and brush, 41.9 x 53.5 cm
The Hague, Royal Library,
inv. 128 A 34

next to the little tower on Hofvijver Lake. The Hague architects turned to treatises by Italian architects such as Palladio (1505-1580) and Scamozzi (1552-1616) for their pilasters, capitals, cornices and tympana, as well as for guidance with the ideal proportions of a building. They were aware that these principles were themselves based on the work of the Roman architect Vitruvius who lived in first century BC. Van Campen and Huygens were both responsible for the plans on which Johan Maurits's house was based, but once the actual building had begun they were assisted by Pieter Post. Post designed (part of?) the interior decoration and in 1652 made a set of drawings with cross-sections, floor plans, elevations and a plan for the decoration of the walls of the Mauritshuis. These are the only surviving impressions of the interior [fig. 7]. The only knowledge we have of the layout of the various rooms comes down to us through an inventory and a description written in 1681 by the painter Jacob de Hennin (1629-after 1688). In his account he expresses his amazement at the strange world to be found inside. The vestibule was decorated with murals of Brazilian landscapes and in the Great Hall on the first floor (now the Potter Room) the collection of 'Braziliana' was displayed: consisting of 'naturalia' and 'arteficialia', implements from the West, stuffed animals, hides, musical instruments, Indian weapons, jewellery, shells and corals, ore, precious metals and stones. In 1644 eleven Indians who had come back with Johan Maurits put on a performance of Brazilian dancing in the forecourt of the Mauritshuis. Curiously enough, Johan Maurits was not all that attached to his collections: he considered them equally suitable for use as state and business presentations, which led to the King of Denmark being given a series of paintings representing Indians and still lifes with fruits from the region. These pictures are now the pride of the ethnographic department of the Statens Museum for Kunst in Copenhagen. As early as 1652 he had already sold quite a number of items to the Grand Elector of Brandenburg (1620-1688), including 800 sketches of fruits, plants, fishes, reptiles, birds, insects, mammals, Indians and mulattos. In 1679, shortly before his death, Johan Maurits made Louis XIV (1638-1715) a gift of a collection of 'Braziliana'.

Johan Maurits's aspirations went beyond The Hague. His personal motto was 'Qua patet orbis' (to the end of the earth). In 1647 Johan

[8]

After Bartholomeus Eggers,
c.1630-1692
*Bust of Johan Maurits (1604-1679),
Count of Nassau-Siegen, founder of
the Mauritshuis*
Inv. KN 20 (copy after the original
dated 1664 in the Fürstengruft,
Siegen)

[9]

Pierre Phillipe, died 1664, after
Jacob Toorenvliet, 1635/6-1719
*Banquet in the Mauritshuis on
the occasion of the visit of Charles II,
King of England, 30 May 1660*,
c.1660
Engraving, 40 x 49 cm
Inv. 1087

[10]

Illustration from Jean Bérain,
*100 Planches principales de l'œuvre
complet de Jean Bérain 1649-1711*,
Paris 1882

14

Maurits was appointed Stadholder of Cleves by the Grand Elector of Brandenburg, who in 1646 had married a daughter of Frederik Hendrik and Amalia of Solms. In Cleves he laid out extensive gardens and commissioned the building of the Freudenburg summer estate and the so-called amphitheatre [compare fig. 1]. Thanks to the changes brought about in the landscape by Johan Maurits, Cleves came to be known as the garden city. Despite all his political activities, Johan Maurits managed to reside at The Hague at regular intervals and occasionally let others have the freedom of his house. To mention but one notable occasion, the Great Hall on the first floor of the Mauritshuis was used for a farewell banquet held in honour of Charles II [fig. 9] in 1660. Johan Maurits was appointed to the rank of Field Marshall by the Republic of the Netherlands in 1668. In that year Maurits Post (1645-1677) – Pieter Post's son – produced a completely new design for the garden of the Mauritshuis including a bust dedicated to its founder to be placed at the very end of the park. The bust in the Mauritshuis [fig. 8] is a modern replica of this original, which was placed in Johan Maurits's tomb in Siegen. He died in Bergendael near Cleves, on the 20th of December 1679. After Johan Maurits's death his house in The Hague passed into the hands of the Maes family, who had served as his principal money lender; they subsequently leased the building. On the night of the 23rd and 24th of December 1704 the interior went up in flames. A certain Willem Wolf had wanted to warm up the house for the secretary of the Duke of Marlborough, who was then staying there. Wolf had been drinking to reduce the tedium of his task and must have forgotten to snuff out the candle in one of the rooms, where, as a result, a crate of champagne packed in straw, caught fire. The bottles exploded, and the fire which subsequently broke out destroyed everything but the main structure of the building.

Fortunately it was decided to restore the building rather than demolishing it to make way for the erection of a new one. It was hoped that a lottery would raise the necessary funds but the proceeds were rather disappointing. Nevertheless, between 1708 and 1718, both the interior and exterior of the building were gradually restored and the house was renovated to include all the facilities needed to make it into a modern residence. The most significant result was that the rooms became considerably lighter: the windows were elongated, the

The Golden Room with paintings by Giovanni Antonio
Pellegrini (1675-1741), completed in 1718

walls originally separating the stairs from the vestibule were not
reinstated, thus creating a more spacious effect in the entrance hall;
the upper room was adorned with white stucco decorations. Gijsbert
Blotelingh, master mason in The Hague, was in charge of
the restoration. The design of his mantelpieces came largely from
sample books [fig. 10] by the French architect Jean Bérain (1637-1711).
Giovanni Antonio Pellegrini (1675-1741), the Venetian artist who
happened to be passing through The Hague in 1718, was commissioned
to execute the decorative paintings in the Golden Room. He made

a number of murals and ceiling paintings depicting allegorical subjects in the late Louis XIV style [fig. 11]. The drum and cupola motif (depicted in the print of c.1660, see fig. 9) disappeared from the Great Hall on the first floor (now the Potter Room). In 1910 the moulded ceiling was in turn replaced by decorative paintings by Jacob de Wit (1695-1754), originating from a house in Leiden.

In the early eighteenth century the Mauritshuis still served as a residence for ambassadors; it later came to be used as a military school; the cellars were leased to a wine merchant and after 1795 it even stooped to housing political prisoners. In 1807 the Mauritshuis regained something of its former glory when the Royal Library was established there. However, within less than ten years, the library had already outgrown its premises. In 1820 the former house of Johan Maurits was purchased by the Dutch State to accommodate the Royal Cabinet of Paintings (on the first floor) and Curiosities (on the ground floor, until 1875). On 3 January 1822 the State Newspaper made the following announcement: 'From now on the Royal Cabinet of Paintings in The Hague can be visited on Wednesdays and Saturdays from 10 am to 1 pm by anyone who is well dressed and not accompanied by children'. This move meant that the monumental building had become a museum, excluding all other functions.

A ROYAL INSTITUTION

In the early hours of the 18th of January 1795 Stadholder Willem V (1748-1806) fled to England with his family. The Republic of the United Provinces was about to become the Batavian Republic. The country's major art treasures were confiscated by the French occupying forces as spoils of war. Among these were some 200 pictures which together formed the 'Cabinet du Stathouder' in The Hague. They were taken to Paris in June 1795. Mercifully, the Batavian House of Representatives was granted the sabre of Michiel de Ruyter (1607-1676), the baton of Maarten Tromp (1598-1653) and a few other items of historical interest belonging to Willem V. For 20 years the French were able to gaze at *The bull* [fig. p. 109] by Paulus Potter (1625-1654) which had been hung in the Louvre between the Raphaels and Titians looted from Italy. After Napoleon's abdication in 1814 and the Battle

[12]

D.L.M. van Valkenburg, active *c.*1839
The return of the Stadholder's pictures in
The Hague, 14 November 1815, 1839
Pen in brown and brush, 9.6 x 15.7 cm
The Hague, Gemeentearchief, inv. kl. A 113

of Waterloo in 1815 the return of the stolen works of art was demanded
through diplomatic channels. Their return followed promptly. On the
14th of November 1815 a triumphal procession of volunteers from The
Hague, 20 cavalrymen and numerous dignitaries entered the Buitenhof
in The Hague with the 120 recovered paintings loaded on wagons,
accompanied by cannon fire and peals of bells [fig. 12]. The bulk of
the collection, that had once belonged to the Stadholder was home
again. Unfortunately, at least 70 paintings were permanently left in
France. Thus one may nowadays come across oddly displaced pictures
in French provincial museums: in Lyon the *Portrait of Willem III (1650-*
1702) in a floral wreath by Jan Davidsz de Heem (1606-1683/4) and
in Rennes *The wedding of Friedrich Wilhelm (1620-1688) and Louise*
Henriette of Orange-Nassau (1627-1667) by Jan Mijtens (*c.*1614-1670).

During the Batavian Republic a core collection of books had been
assembled and institutionalised as a National Library. In 1807, in the
reign of Louis Napoleon (1778-1846), this collection was transferred
to the Mauritshuis, where it came to be known as the Royal Library.

More or less as a continuation of this policy King Willem I (1772-1843), who was proclaimed sovereign ruler in 1813, founded several national institutions which were to house, among other things, his father's reclaimed collections. On Stadholder Willem V's death in 1806, his books and manuscripts transferred ownership and became the property of the Royal Library, which was housed in the Mauritshuis. In 1816 the Royal Coin Cabinet was to be established there too. A number of treasures which Willem V had taken to England, and a collection of inherited Japanese and Chinese objects, formed the nucleus of the Royal Cabinet of Curiosities, which was housed in several rooms of what had formerly been 'Willem V's Cabinet' in the Buitenhof. The gallery now came to be used as an exhibition area for the Stadholder's pictures, which had been handed over to the Dutch State unofficially with the establishment of the Royal Cabinet of Paintings. In 1822 both collections were transferred to the Mauritshuis.

Johan Steengracht van Oostkapelle (1782-1846) was made honorary director of the picture gallery and the painter Jan Willem Pieneman (1779-1853) was given the salaried post of deputy director. From 1817 the collection was open to the public for two days a week. The rest of the time was reserved for experts wishing to study the pictures and for artists who wanted to make copies of them. During Steengracht's regime an illustrated catalogue was published in four volumes between 1826 and 1830, which included descriptions highlighting 100 pictures from the collection with reproductions in steel engraving. The royal family's concern for the well-being of the Royal Cabinet can be seen from the dedication in Steengracht's catalogue: 'à sa Majesté la Reine des Pays-Bas, protectrice des beaux-arts'. With due pride he concluded the selection of 100 masterpieces from the Mauritshuis in 1830 with a reproduction of *The anatomy lesson of Dr Nicolaes Tulp* [fig. p. 113] by Rembrandt (1606-1669), which had been added to the collection only a short time before. In 1828 Willem I had in fact acquired the painting for 'his' museum after issuing a Royal Decree preventing the public sale of the work. Actually, he often gave explicit instructions like these about the purchase of a particular piece and apparently had special funds for this purpose, presumably drawn from his own private income.

To illustrate this, we see that in 1820 the King had bought the portrait of Paulus Potter, which had been painted posthumously by Bartholomeus van der Helst (1613-1670). He bought it at an auction of the property of a descendant of the artist of *The bull*. From then on all major purchases made by the government were sent to The Hague by the King. In this way, on the 11th of June 1822 the director of the Rijksmuseum in Amsterdam, Cornelis Apostool (1752-1844), was to promise the director of the Mauritshuis that he would send him the *View of Delft* [fig. p. 145] by Johannes Vermeer (1632-1675), which had been bought at the Stinstra sale shortly before. This was also how the *View of Haarlem with bleaching grounds* [fig. p. 125] by Jacob van Ruisdael (1628/9-1682) found its way into the Hague collection in 1827. *The lamentation of Christ* [fig. p. 149] by Rogier van der Weyden (c.1399-1464) – at the time attributed to Hans Memling (1435/40-1491) – was purchased by Willem I personally from Baron Keverberg van Kessel in Brussels. This might be regarded as a historic act, as the piece is one of the few major examples of early Flemish painting housed in Holland. Four of the paintings which established the fame of the Mauritshuis – *The anatomy lesson of Dr Nicolaes Tulp*, the *View of Delft*, the *View of Haarlem with bleaching grounds* and *The lamentation of Christ* – entered the collection through the patronage of Willem I.

The Belgian Uprising caused widespread financial difficulty, the effects of which were even felt in the Royal Cabinet in The Hague. From 1832 no further purchases were made for the museum and under King Willem II (1792-1849) no one took the slightest interest in the institution. In 1850 and 1851 Willem II's private collection, including the most beautiful fifteenth and sixteenth-century masterpieces, was put up for auction. None of these pictures went to the Mauritshuis, which for years had to make do with a budget which amounted to no more than 810 guilders.

It is only since about 1874 that the collection has really been able to expand through purchases made from state funds, bequests from private individuals and long-term loans. The museum has always tried to acquire paintings of special quality or interest, thereby following the pattern set by Willem I. Today the Mauritshuis can be said to house a royal collection of paintings, both in a historical and artistic sense.

From the outset King Willem I housed the Royal Cabinet of Paintings and that of Curiosities together in the Mauritshuis. It was not until 1875 that the whole of the building became available for the picture collection which from then on grew steadily. In 1874 Victor de Stuers (1843-1916) published a new catalogue which incorporated 318 paintings and 15 sculptures. In the opening lines of his preface he stated that the Hague museum had become one of Europe's most remarkable galleries, not because it housed so many paintings, but because of their outstanding quality. Quality has been the most important factor in the museum's acquisition policy ever since. Benefactors of the Mauritshuis have respected this aim, as can be witnessed by the many donations of exceptional quality over the years.

Many of the pictures bequeathed by the stadholders have found their way into the Mauritshuis. In the case of the *Portrait of Floris van Egmond (1469-1539)* [fig. p. 75] by Jan Gossaert (1478-1532) the direct provenance is from Anna van Buren (1533-1558), who married Willem of Orange, but can be traced right back to the sitter himself. The walls of the vestibule in the Mauritshuis are hung with portraits of the stadholders and their relatives, not because these pictures are of exceptional artistic merit, but because they originate mostly from residences and country houses of the Orange family. The Stadholder's collection sustained a number of heavy losses when Amalia of Solms's pictures were divided among her four daughters, who all married German princes. Rembrandt's well-known Passion-series, which had been painted at Frederik Hendrik's special request, thus found its way to Germany. In 1713, due to financial difficulties, part of the collection belonging to Het Loo Palace was put op for auction in Amsterdam. Among the works that were sold on this occasion was *Vertumnus and Pomona* by Peter Paul Rubens (1577-1640) and Jan Brueghel the Elder (1568-1625). In the course of the eighteenth century Willem IV (1711-1751) and Willem V managed to some extent to make amends for the two big gaps which had been left in the collection. At any rate, one might interpret the acquisition of Rembrandt's *Simeon's song of praise* [fig. p. 111] in 1773, and Rubens's en Jan Brueghel's *Garden of Eden with the fall of Man* [fig. p. 55] in 1766, as a kind of reparation.

When country houses were pulled down around The Hague, the official portraits they had previously housed found a suitable home in the Mauritshuis too: the *Portrait of Willem III (1650-1702) as a child with his aunt Maria of Nassau (1642-1688)* by Gerard van Honthorst (1590-1656), for example, had originally hung in Huis ten Bosch Palace, whilst his *Portrait of Stadholder Frederik Hendrik (1584-1647) and his wife Amalia of Solms (1602-1675)* [fig. 4] came from Constantijn Huygens's house. *Theagenes receiving the palm of honour from Charicleia* [fig. p. 45] by Abraham Bloemaert (1564-1651) was painted in 1626 in commission from Frederik Hendrik on the occasion of his marriage to Amalia of Solms. Large-scale decorative pieces in the present collection are *Zeus as a child on Crete* [fig. p. 41] by Nicolaes Berchem (1620-1683) and *Mercury, Argus and Io* by Jacob van Campen, the architect of the Mauritshuis.

Several pictures in the collection belonged at one time to the English royal family. *The young mother* [fig. p. 63] by Gerrit Dou (1613-1675), one of the pictures that was presented to Charles II with the 'Dutch Gift', was taken back to Holland by Stadholder Willem III (1650-1702) after his accession to the English throne in 1688. The painting was subsequently added to the collection of the renovated Het Loo Palace. The *Portrait of Robert Cheseman (1485-1547)* [fig. p. 89] by Hans Holbein the Younger (1497/8-1543) and other portraits by the court painter of Henry VIII (1491-1547) came to the Netherlands in the same way, which later gave rise to protests from Queen Anne: but to no avail.

The Mauritshuis seems to have a number of paintings which were either made for or later acquired by the stadholders. There are two closely connected motives which underlie the Orange's collecting activities in the eighteenth century: family pride and national sentiment. One of the reasons for the hereditary Stadholder Willem IV purchasing Paulus Potter's *Bull* in 1749 was that it was then considered to be 'his most striking work known in the country'. From 1760 the court was once again actively involved in the (national) art market. A special acquisition was *The tomb of Willem of Orange in Delft* [fig. p. 93] by Gerard Houckgeest (c.1600-1661). Willem V was 16 years old when he bought this picture in 1764. The image of this national monument had, of course, a special appeal for him and it was his interest in

[13]

Antoon François Heijligers, 1828-1897
*Interior of the Rembrandt Room in
the Mauritshuis*, 1884
Panel, 47 x 59 cm
Inv. 1055

history which again persuaded him to buy the so-called *'Poultry yard'*
[fig. p. 133] by Jan Steen (1626-1679) ten years later. The salesman
wilfully led him to believe that one of the Princesses of Orange was
depicted in it. Likewise, *Diogenes looking for an honest man* [fig. p. 67]
by Caesar van Everdingen (*c.*1617-1678) was supposed to include the
ancestors of Pieter Steyn (1706-1772), the personal advisor of Willem V.

As has already been mentioned, the Stadholder's collection was
opened to the public in 1774. Hundred years later the Royal Cabinet
of Pictures had become the sole occupant of the Mauritshuis.
Meanwhile, as De Stuers so rightly observed in 1874, it had acquired
the reputation of a great museum. In 1884 Antoon François Heijligers
(1828-1897) painted the *Interior of the Rembrandt Room in the Mauritshuis*
[fig. 13]. *The bull* and *The anatomy lesson of Dr Nicolaes Tulp* were
major tourist attractions which, in particular, attracted many foreign

visitors to The Hague. The well-known French critic Thoré-Bürger (1807-1869) came to The Hague to study the great masters of the Golden Age and through his writings even came to be known as the rediscoverer of Vermeer. In rather dramatic terms he described his long journey to The Hague and the endless formalities he had been put through to obtain a photograph of the *View of Delft*.

The Mauritshuis lived up to this new status both in its choice of new acquisitions and in the publication of scholarly catalogues. After the appointment of Abraham Bredius (1855-1946) to the post of director in 1889, the collection was once again enriched with interesting pieces on a regular basis. In 1894 Bredius was in London, where he bought the completely unknown *Portrait of a man from the Lespinette family*, then alleged to be by Antonello da Messina (*c.*1430-1479) but now attributed to Memling [fig. p. 97]. Experts agreed that he had managed to buy it for much less than its actual value. In the same vein, Bredius found himself in Paris in 1896 with a budget of no more than a few thousand guilders when *The goldfinch* [fig. p. 69] by Carel Fabritius (1622-1654) came up for auction there. Afterwards he proudly described how he had asked a friend to do the bidding so that his interest in the picture would not push up the price.

Meanwhile the collection in the Mauritshuis was also endowed with various bequests. An important event was the acquisition of 25 pictures from Bredius's own collection which for many years had been hanging in the museum on loan. Among these were Rembrandt's *Homer* [fig. p. 117] as well as *Saul and David* and *Two moors*. Through another bequest, in 1903, the Mauritshuis came into possession of several masterpieces, including Johannes Vermeer's *Girl with a pearl earring* [fig. p. 147], which is one of the public's favourites. The picture was bequeathed by A.A. des Tombe, who had bought it for less than two guilders and fifty cents in 1882. Des Tombe also left the museum the beautiful *Vase with flowers in a niche* [fig. p. 49] by Ambrosius Bosschaert (1573-1621). In 1936 Sir Henry Deterding made the museum a major donation: among the works was the *'Oyster-eater'* [fig. p. 131] by Jan Steen. In 1909 Wilhelm Martin (1876-1854) succeeded Bredius to the post of director. During his directorship, in 1913, the Steengracht Collection came op for auction in Paris. This collection comprised seventeenth-century masterpieces which for a long time had been on display in a house on the Vijverberg, where they competed for the visitor's attention with the treasures in the Mauritshuis. Fortunately the Rembrandt Society had been founded by this time, on private initiative, which would intervene to buy works of art whenever the government, out of phillistinism, refused. Supplemented by contributions from the royal family and many private individuals, the Rembrandt Society secured five paintings for the Mauritshuis which resulted in the government eventually feeling compelled to grant additional funds for purchasing. The museum thus acquired *Hunting for lice* [fig. p. 47] by Gerard ter Borch (1617-1681) and *'The way you hear it, is the way you sing it'* [fig. p. 135] by Jan Steen. A similar financial joint-venture was called for to buy *Travellers outside an inn* [fig. p. 105] by Isack van Ostade (1621-1649), a painting which in fact came from the famous Wallace Collection in London. Martin was proud of this acquisition.

After the second World War the Mauritshuis collection was augmented with a number of pictures which, after original confiscation, had been recovered from Germany. In this way several masterpieces from what had formerly been the Mannheimer Collection found their way into the museum: the *View of the Oudezijds Voorburgwal with the Bierkaai and the Oude Kerk in Amsterdam* [fig. p. 85] by Jan van der Heyden (1637-1712) – a picture with an eventful past – and the delicately painted *Brothel scene* [fig. p. 101] by Frans van Mieris the Elder (1635-1681). In 1947 the museum purchased Rembrandt's last self-portrait [fig. p. 121] from the Rathenau family – it had been on loan to the Rijksmuseum before the war. Such exceptional pictures befitted the reputation the Mauritshuis had acquired both with the public and with connoisseurs of art.

Over the last decades the buying policy has remained in line with the trend set by King Willem I: always to endeavour to acquire pieces of exceptional significance – preferably from the Golden Age – without trying to make the collection 'complete'. With the acquisition of Rubens's *'Modello' for The assumption of Mary* [fig. p. 123] and *The adoration of the shepherds* [fig. p. 95] by Jacob Jordaens (1593-1678) an extra dimension was added to the collection. In return for the Italian and several Spanish and French pictures which were given on long-term loan to the Rijksmuseum, the Mauritshuis received Flemish and

Interior of the Gallery Prince Willem V at the
Buitenhof, reopened in 1977. Here paintings of
the Mauritshuis and loans from the Netherlands
Institute for Cultural Heritage and the
Rijksmuseum are displayed in an eighteenth-
century fashion: frame to frame, covering nearly
the entire wall (present situation).

some German paintings from the fifteenth and sixteenth centuries,
a few seventeenth-century Flemish masterworks and a collection
of miniatures. In this way the *Portrait of Francesco Giamberti
(1405-1480)* and the *Portrait of Giuliano da San Gallo (1445-1516)*
by Piero di Cosimo (1461/2-c.1521) went to Amsterdam, while Jan
Gossaert's *Portrait of Floris van Egmond (1469-1539)* [fig. p. 75] came
to The Hague.

Time and again the Friends of the Mauritshuis Foundation has given invaluable support to help the museum purchase paintings. It was largely thanks to a very substantial contribution by the Foundation that the museum was able to buy, in 1999, the *Portrait of an elderly man* by Rembrandt (1606-1669), signed and dated 1667 [fig. p. 119]. Rembrandt's portrayal of the old man, about whose identity we are as yet wholly in the dark, is extremely striking. The acquisition of this painting – one of the finest and best preserved portraits from the master's final years – is without question a great day in the history of the Mauritshuis. Since the Foundation's acquisition of *Simeon's song of praise* [fig. p. 73] by Arent de Gelder (1645-1727) and *Isaac and Rebecca* by Gerbrand van den Eeckhout (1621-1674) in 1987 and 1989 respectively, Rembrandt's pupils finally have the place they deserve in the Mauritshuis. In 1994 the museum was able to acquire *The old lace worker* by Nicolaes Maes (1634-1693), who is also regarded as one of Rembrandt's most important pupils. It is a painting that is undoubtedly seen at its best in the museum's intimate atmosphere. A generous donation by the Onderlinge Levensverzekering-Maatschappij ''s-Graven-hage' in 1995 enabled the Mauritshuis to display for the first time a genre scene by Gerard van Honthorst (1590-1656). The three genre pieces by this artist that Napoleon seized in 1795 as part of the stad-holder's collection were never returned. Van Honthorst's superb *Violin player* from 1626 [fig. p. 91] is a typical example of the work of the Utrecht Caravaggists, very few of whose works can be seen in The Hague.

The *Vase with flowers* [fig. p. 83] by Jan Davidsz de Heem (1606-1683/4), which the Foundation purchased in 1993, is an important addition to the museum's still-life collection. De Heem, whose flower pieces are rare, is one of the most versatile still-life painters of the Golden Age. In 1995 Mrs Edward Speelman donated to the museum, in memory of her husband, Mr Edward Joseph Speelman, the extremely elegant *Still life with strawberries* [fig. p. 61] by Adriaen Coorte (active *c.*1683-1707), the true value of whose oeuvre has only been appreciated in the last few decades. A year later, the museum acquired the *Flower still life with shells* by Balthasar van der Ast (1593/4-1657) from the estate of *jonkheer* John H. Loudon, former president of the Foundation. The painting had already been shown in the Mauritshuis at the successful exhibition *The Mauritshuis in bloom: Bouquets from* *the Golden Age* (1992). These three acquisitions have enabled visitors to the museum to gain a far better understanding of the way in which flower pieces evolved over time.

At the end of 1994, the Mauritshuis acquired the *Wooded landscape with cottages* [fig. p. 87] by Meindert Hobbema (1638-1709) at a London auction. The painting, which could not have been purchased without the support of many donors, is the first work by Hobbema in a Dutch public collection that displays his qualities to the full. To date, the painting is the first example in the Mauritshuis of a monumental Dutch landscape from the seventeenth century. Gaps in the collection in the area of the Italianate painters – specialising in southern land-scapes – have also been filled, thanks to the acquisition of paintings by Bartholomeus Breenbergh (1598-1657), Pieter van Laer (1599-after 1642) and Dirck van der Lisse (1607-1657), as well as loans of a number of paintings by the Netherlands Institute for Cultural Heritage in 1992.

A touching show of public support ensued in response to a plea in the press in 1992 for the acquisition of the *Portrait of Constantijn Huygens (1596-1687) and Suzanna van Baerle (1599-1637)* by Jacob van Campen [fig. p. 59] for the Mauritshuis. Thanks to many gifts, and that of one private individual in particular, this portrait could be pur-chased at auction. In the same period the *Trompe-l'oeil with a bust of Venus* from 1665 by Caesar van Everdingen (*c.*1617-1678) was donated to the museum by a private individual. Van Everdingen is one of the leading exponents of Dutch Classicist painting. That private initiative is particularly well-disposed to the Mauritshuis was proved yet again in 1997, when a faithful friend of the museum gave the Foundation a considerable sum to help it purchase *The adoration of the shepherds* from 1665 by Jan de Bray (*c.*1627-1697). This intimate painting [fig. p. 51] by the Haarlem classicist master is a welcome addition to the collection of history pieces. Also in 1997, a private individual donated two fine paintings to the museum. They are arcadian landscapes by Jan van Huysum (1682-1749) dating from 1724-1725 [figs. 15-16]. The pendants were produced in the first half of the eighteenth century, a period to which art historians have been devoting more attention in recent years. With all these acquisitions, the Mauritshuis, which has also been pursuing an active exhibition policy for some years now, has been able to improve its collection to no small extent.

[15-16]
Jan van Huysum, 1682-1749
Arcadian landscape with bust of Flora (top) and
*Arcadian landscape with the healing of the crippled man
by Peter and John* (bottom), 1724-1725
Canvas, each 52 x 71 cm
Inv. 1113-1114 (permanent loan from the Friends of
the Mauritshuis Foundation)

29

SELECTION

of highlights in the Mauritshuis
(in alphabetical order)

Willem van Aelst signed and dated this still life 'Guill.ᵐᵒ van Aelst 1663', the Italianised first name referring to the period 1645-1656 that he spent in Tuscany in the service of Ferdinand II de' Medici (1610-1670), Grand Duke of Tuscany. The artist worked in Amsterdam from 1657 onwards, where he would sign with his Italianised signature exclusively.

Van Aelst played an important part in the development of the flower still life. He was one of the first painters to abandon the symmetrical composition that had prevailed hitherto as well as the traditional frontal illumination. His bouquets, in contrast, display a diagonal arrangement in combination with strong light-dark contrasts.
   This bouquet from 1663 is one of the most expressive examples of his work. The flowers are arranged along a diagonal that runs from the red and white carnation at lower left to the red poppy at upper right. Some of the flowers at the centre of the composition are fully illumi-nated – the orange African marigold, the Guelder rose

and the Provence rose – while others, such as the soft red Damascene rose, are left in the shadows. The harmonious mix of warm and cool colours extends to the marble surface and the silver vase, executed in the so-called auricular style.

The open watch recalling the passage of time was the attribute *par excellence* to add a note of vanitas to a flower still life. On further inspection we indeed discover that many of the leaves have been attacked by insects or a plant virus. The bluebottle that stands out against the white Guelder rose in the centre of the composition was sometimes used to symbolise the brevity of life.

Willem van Aelst, 1627-after 1683

Flower still life with watch, 1663

Canvas, 62.5 x 49 cm

Inv. 2

This still life is unique in the oeuvre of Pieter van Anraadt, both in quality and in choice of subject. For this Deventer artist chiefly produced portraits, which are greatly inferior in quality to this immensely attractive still life.

Van Anraadt probably took his inspiration from similar images by the Amsterdam painters Jan Jansz den Uyl (1595/6-1639/40), Jan Jansz Treck (c.1606-1652?) and Jan Jansz van de Velde (c.1619-1663). But in their work we shall seek in vain for the astonishing rendering of light that Van Anraadt has contrived to achieve here. His depiction of the earthenware jug commands particular admiration.

In the seventeenth century still life paintings of this kind were often referred to as 'a beer and baccy' ('een biertie met een toebackje'). A small number of objects are arrayed on the corner of a cloth-draped table: an earthenware jug, a glass of beer, a coal pan with burning coals and a dish containing tobacco and a few pipes.

Van Anraadt probably wished to convey the four elements here: earth (the jug), water (the main ingredient of beer), fire (the coals) and air (which is inhaled through the pipes). Van Anraadt's father-in-law, the poet Jan van der Veen (1578-1659), published a book of poems in 1653 entitled *Raadtselen* (Riddles). It includes a poem that may be translated as follows:

> An EARTHEN POT
> is the answer here,
>
> Made of water,
> fire and clay,
>
> Then dried to a
> finish by the air,
>
> Four elements
> all in sway.

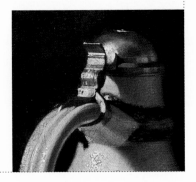

Pieter van Anraadt, *c.*1635-1678

Still life with earthenware jug and pipes, 1658

Canvas, 67 x 59 cm
Inv. 1045

In this early still life Balthasar van der Ast choose a relatively high vantage point, resulting in a clearly structured composition in which each element is easily identifiable. Our attention is drawn to the fruit displayed on a Ming dish – two large yellow quinces, surrounded by two pomegranates, apricots and bunches of grapes. Spread out on the tablecloth are pears, apricots, an orange, shells and a tulip. A 'painted lady' is crawling along the tulip stem while a red admiral has alighted on the edge of the table. In addition to these butterflies, we also find a dragonfly and a fly on one of the quinces, a grasshopper on the vine and an earwig in the grapes.

The painter may have added these insects to underscore the ephemeral nature of this luscious fruit – which further inspection indeed reveals to be already showing signs of decay – and hence of life in general. The fly in particular was seen as symbolising the brevity of life. The butterfly, on the other hand, which had come forth from a caterpillar, often stood for life after death in this context. Finally, the shells may have been intended as allusions to the vanity of human efforts to gain earthly possessions: at the beginning of the seventeenth century they were sold for exorbitant prices.

Van der Ast was trained as a painter by his brother-in-law Ambrosius Bosschaert the Elder (see pp. 48-49). From 1619 to 1632 he worked in Utrecht, after which he moved to Delft. His oeuvre displays a dazzling variety, from large, intricate bouquets and baskets of flowers, to compositions featuring one or a small group of flowers or shells. The Mauritshuis owns several paintings by Van der Ast.

Balthasar van der Ast, 1593/4-1657

Fruit still life with shells, 1620

Panel, 46 x 64.5 cm
Inv. 1066

A frozen canal in a peasant village provides the setting for this winter scene by Hendrick Avercamp, the first artist to specialise in the drawing and painting of typical Dutch scenes on the ice. Paying particular attention to anecdotal details he painted numerous little figures from all walks of life, as is clear from their meticulously rendered costumes. In the foreground, our eye is caught by a richly dressed skater with a plumed top hat. Couples glide over the ice hand in hand, a group is playing *kolf* (a forerunner of today's ice hockey) and a woman is doing the washing in a hole in the ice near a waterlogged rowing boat. An amusing detail is the bare buttocks under the skirts of a woman who has taken a tumble, but Avercamp also points out the more serious hazards of this winter recreation. Near the left bank, four people have fallen through the ice. The lift bridge marks the transition to the expansive ice panorama, where the silhouette of the town stretches across the horizon.

This panel by 'the mute from Kampen' – Avercamp is assumed to have been deaf and dumb – was probably produced around 1610, when the painter may have returned to Kampen after his apprenticeship in Amsterdam. It still displays the influence of the Flemish landscape tradition that had developed in Antwerp since Pieter Bruegel the Elder (1520/25-1569) and which enjoyed a final resurgence of glory in the northern Netherlands – especially in Amsterdam – after the arrival of Flemish immigrants around 1600. Characteristic features include the high decorative tree as a foreground coulisse, the stage-like composition, the painting's many colourful details and its anecdotal quality. The theme of the winter landscape with people enjoying themselves on the ice originates in the sixteenth-century Flemish tradition of the rendering of the months and seasons.

Hendrick Avercamp, 1585-1634

*On the ice, c.*1610

Panel, 36 x 71 cm
Inv. 785
(long-term loan from the Rijksmuseum, Amsterdam)

The infant Zeus is hidden by his mother Rhea on mount Ida on Crete because she fears the child's father Cronus, who devours his children for fear of being supplanted. There the child is brought up by the princess Adrastea, who feeds him on honey, and by the goat Amalthea, who gives him her milk to drink. Berchem has depicted the three in the company of a sheep, an ass and a recumbent cow. A grinning faun is approaching with a vat of milk. Zeus is lying asleep in the lap of the beautiful Adrastea. His pose is derived from a well-known sculpture by Artus Quellinus (1609-1668), a sculptor who was very popular at the court in The Hague.

Artus Quellinus, 1609-1668
Cupid sleeping, 1641
Ivory, length 11.6 cm
Baltimore, The Walters Art Gallery

The theme of the raising of Zeus is based on examples by Jacob Jordaens (pp. 94-95), who was also admired in courtly circles in The Hague. The merry faun is a familiar figure in the work of the Flemish painter.

When Berchem painted this vast canvas in 1648, he was being considered as a candidate for the Oranjezaal decorations in Huis ten Bosch Palace in The Hague, to commemorate Stadholder Frederik Hendrik (p. 10, fig. 4), deceased in 1647. Berchem specialised in small, idealised landscapes with staffage, and in producing this painting he may have been trying to show he was perfectly capable of executing large-scale wall decorations as well. The painter did not receive the coveted commission, however. He made up his will in 1649, while preparing for the customary art tour of Italy where he stayed until 1653.

Nicolaes Berchem, 1620-1683

Zeus as a child on Crete, 1648

Canvas, 202 x 262 cm

Inv. 11

This colourful market scene in an oriental or Roman port depicts the biblical story of the calling of Matthew. The New Testament relates: 'And as Jesus passed forth from thence, he saw a man, named Matthew, sitting at the receipt of custom: and he saith unto him, follow me. And he arose, and followed him' (Matthew 9: 9). Jesus towers over the crowd and points with outstretched arm to the man whom tradition describes as a publican. The book in his lap does not refer to any profits of usury; instead, we can just make out the names of the two painters who took credit for the work: 'Berchem gemaek(t) Weenix (ge)daen' (made by Berchem, done by Weenix).

The fact that two artists colla-borated on this painting made it a much coveted collector's item in its day. However, it is not easy to establish what part each played in the whole – it is quite different from an elaborate landscape by one artist in which the other simply added a number of figures. We do have a few significant clues to help us. The man with the black hair and red cloak who stands exactly at the precise intersection of the diagonals resembles a drawn portrait by Berchem, who was an adept figure painter (pp. 40-41). The group at the front on the left, with the sheep, the goat and the lamb, turns up almost identically in a painting by Jan Baptist Weenix, who is also known as a painter of cattle. All in all it seems most likely that Weenix painted most of the scene, starting at the back and working towards the front – after which Berchem finished it by depicting the group of figures around Christ.

Nicolaes Berchem, 1620-1683
Jan Baptist Weenix, 1621-1660/1

The calling of Matthew, c.1657-1660

Panel, 94.2 x 116 cm

Inv. 1058

In a commission for Stadholder Frederik Hendrik (1584-1647) to commemorate his marriage to Amalia of Solms (1602-1675) in 1625, the Utrecht painter Abraham Bloemaert produced a series of paintings depicting episodes from the story of Theagenes and Charicleia. The tale was described in ornate style in *Historiae Aethiopicae*, a popular romance that provided ideal subject matter for decorating palaces, especially when some reference was needed to a wedding. The series by Bloemaert, including this painting in the Mauritshuis, was originally intended for Honselaarsdijk Palace near The Hague.

Bloemaert kept to the text of the romance quite closely, having no doubt been instructed to do so by Frederik Hendrik. Charicleia is born white because her mother, an Ethiopian queen, conceives her while poring in adoration over a picture of the snow-white Andromeda. Her mother conceals her out of fear with a priest in Delphi, on the condition that the girl remains a virgin. After many years, Theagenes, a descendant of Achilles, takes part in the Pythic games at Delphi. As we see in the left background of the painting, he wins the foot race. When accepting the palm from Charicleia, Theagenes kisses her hand, kindling the fire of love in both their hearts. This moment is chosen for the central event in this scene. The lovers decide to seek Chariclea's parents in distant Africa. On their peregrinations they are shipwrecked, fall into the hands of pirates and are taken captive by Ethiopians. All these exhausting adventures are eventually resolved in a happy ending.

Abraham Bloemaert, 1564-1651

Theagenes receiving the palm of honour from Charicleia, 1626

Canvas, 157.2 x 157.7 cm

Inv. 16

One can hardly envisage a more domestic scene than this woman inspecting her child's hair with love and close attention, looking for lice and other vermin. She is totally absorbed in her work while the child – a boy, judging by the smock – waits patiently until she has finished. Gerard ter Borch owes his fame to genre scenes of this kind. In his best works the main character is always totally intent on his or her activity, whether it is reading, making music or some domestic task. The subtle use of light enhances the superb rendering of textures. The figures' faces are often painted with the utmost delicacy, and generally catch the full light, as here.

Aside from visual enjoyment this image also has a wise moral to offer. Seventeenth-century painters and poets saw in the fine-toothed comb a potent symbol of cleanliness, one of the prime virtues of the good housewife. Above an image of a fine-toothed comb in the emblem book *Sinnepoppen* of 1614 by Roemer Pietersz Visscher (1547-1620) is the inscription 'Purgat et ornat' (he cleans and adorns). The popular poet Jacob Cats (1577-1660) had a more profound explanation in mind when he wrote of one whom 'the comb's work on the body put in mind of the need to cleanse the inner man too'.

Gerard ter Borch was born in Zwolle, as the son of the artistically inclined tax collector Gerard ter Borch the Elder (1583-1662), who encouraged his children's artistic aspirations. Gerard's sister Gesina (1631-1690) and brother Moses (1645-1667) were also painters. Besides making genre scenes, Gerard was also a gifted portraitist.

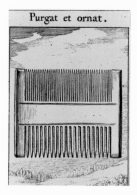

Illustration from Roemer Visscher, *Sinnepoppen*, Amsterdam 1614, no. IX.

Gerard ter Borch, 1617-1681

Hunting for lice, c.1652-1653

Panel, 33.5 x 29 cm

Inv. 744

Bosschaert has placed this bouquet with some thirty different flowers in a window with a view of a panoramic landscape. At the top is a variegated yellow flag iris, and the bouquet also contains African marigolds, garden narcissi, columbines, a snake's head fritillary, forget-me-nots, roses and tulips. It is striking that Bosschaert has depicted the four tulips in this flower piece in different stages of flowering: those at lower left are not yet quite open, those at upper right are in full bloom, while those in the middle are past their first bloom and wilting at the top. Together with the leaves standing out against the blue sky, which have been attacked by disease or insects, this points to a vanitas concept, which Bosschaert has subtly disguised in a superbly painted bouquet.

The same flowers crop up again and again in Bosschaert's bouquets, which indicates that he worked after preliminary drawings. This was sheer necessity for flower painters, as many of the flowers, including those depicted in this painting, bloom at different times. The strictly symmetrical arrangement and even illumination are characteristic of early flower still lifes in the northern Netherlands. This would change completely around 1650 (see Willem van Aelst and Jan Davidsz de Heem, pp. 32-33 and 82-83).

The shells – popular and expensive collector's items – may be a reference to the enormous sums of money that collectors paid for unusual flowers or bulbs at the time. In 1637 this rage, known as 'tulip mania', culminated in a crisis.

Bosschaert spent many years working in Middelburg, where many amateur botanists lived. Later he worked in Bergen op Zoom, Utrecht and Breda. In his signature, a monogram in which the letter 'B' nestles inside the 'A', he emulated the signature of the German Renaissance painter Albrecht Dürer (1471-1528), with whom he may have felt an affinity as an observer of nature.

Ambrosius Bosschaert the Elder, 1573-1621

Vase with flowers in a niche, c.1618

Panel, 64 x 46 cm

Inv. 679

Three shepherds kneel before the newborn Child in the stable at Bethlehem. Joseph places his hand on Mary's back in a protective gesture, while she lifts the sheet and a tiny blanket to show Him to his first worshippers. His crib is a wooden manger – bits of straw poke out from between the planks. The hammer and saw in the left foreground are attributes of Joseph, traditionally described as a carpenter. A crumbling brick wall forms the background against which the Holy Family is depicted. Behind it we can make out the ox and ass in the darkness on the right. The muted colours of this panel are characterised by a range of beige and brown hues, broken only by red and blue accents in Mary's clothes. It is partly this monochrome character that is responsible for the nocturnal intimacy expressed by the scene.

Jan de Bray, who was both history painter and portraitist, painted *The adoration of the shepherds* when he was at the height of his powers.

His works included regents' portraits for the children's poorhouse and lepers' home in Haarlem (now in the Frans Halsmuseum, Haarlem) and large history pieces to decorate buildings such as Haarlem's town hall and Prinsenhof. The golden colouring and clear light of the latter monumental figurative works reflect the classicist tendencies that set the tone in Haarlem paintings from about 1650 onwards.

Aside from these large history pieces, painted on canvas, a few small panels by Jan de Bray are known, primarily with biblical subjects. *The adoration of the shepherds* is a fine example of these more intimate works, and displays De Bray's sure hand at its best.

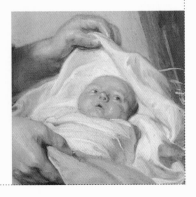

Jan de Bray, *c.*1627-1697

The adoration of the shepherds, 1665

Panel, 63 x 48 cm
Inv. 1110
(permanent loan from the Friends
of the Mauritshuis Foundation, The Hague)

'His beautiful paintings have nothing to show / but the rumpus of men who are playing the fool' wrote Cornelis de Bie (1621/2-1664), Adriaen Brouwer's first biographer, in his *Gulden Cabinet* (1661). 'Playing the fool' obviously relates to Brouwer's choice of subjects: scenes from peasant life, preferably in interiors, with the accent on smoking, drinking, cards and fighting. On the one hand he was following a tradition developed by Pieter Bruegel the Elder (1520/25-1569), and on the other hand he introduced a new element into northern Netherlandish genre paintings, with the rough and unadorned manner in which he depicted his characters.

Brouwer came from Oudenaerde in Flanders. From 1626 to the early 1630s he worked in Haarlem and Amsterdam, and after 1632 he was active in Antwerp. Painters such as Peter Paul Rubens (pp. 132-133) and Rembrandt (pp. 110-121) were great admirers of his work. Rembrandt may well have been captivated by the grimaces of Brouwer's figures, of which the painting discussed here includes several superb examples. The man seated on the left, who is being pulled roughly by the hair, is making fiendish faces, while the man drawing his sword at centre foreground has a particularly bloodthirsty expression. Five others sitting around a table are engrossed in the fight, but the two men sitting on the right carry on chatting as if nothing is happening. The riotousness of the scene is emphasised by the dog mounting a pig in the right foreground and the man in the right background who has crouched down in full public view, if with his back towards us, to defecate.

Adriaen Brouwer, 1606-1638

Peasants fighting, c.1625-1626

Panel, 25 x 34 cm
Inv. 919
(long-term loan from the Rijksmuseum, Amsterdam)

This masterful painting is the result of a collaborative venture by two specialists. Rubens painted the two nude figures while Brueghel executed the landscape and animals. Rubens' wide brushstrokes are clearly distinct from the refined painting that is the hallmark of the 'Velvet' Brueghel. The intensity of the collaboration is clear from a variety of details. The lion and tiger painted by Brueghel, for instance, are quotations from the oeuvre of Rubens. The overall composition, on the other hand, was probably an invention of Brueghel, whose oeuvre contains other similar pieces.

A painting like this was intended first and foremost as a showpiece, the object being to dazzle the viewer with an astounding display of virtuosity. But the painters also incorporated a wealth of symbolism. For instance, the little monkey at far left alludes to Adam's eating of the forbidden fruit, moments away, which will lead to the fall of Man. Monkeys, outwardly akin to humans but without their capacity to distinguish between good and evil, were often used in the seventeenth century to symbolise evil. The brightly illuminated bunch of grapes in the foliage on the left is undoubtedly an allusion to the crucifixion of Christ, which redeemed mankind from the fall.

Jan Brueghel the Elder, 1568-1625
Peter Paul Rubens, 1577-1640

The garden of Eden with the fall of Man, c.1615

Panel, 74.3 x 114.7 cm

Inv. 253

The angel who comes to liberate Peter from captivity brings his shadowed face close to that of the chained old apostle, pointing upward to indicate his divine authority. The light falls on the startled face of Peter, who, with his sunken eye sockets, red nose and toothless mouth is rendered with an almost painful realism. The life-sized half-figures are depicted against a dark background without any staffage, so that there is nothing to distract the viewer's attention from this dramatic meeting.

The deliverance of Peter was a popular theme of Caravaggio (1571-1610) and his Utrecht followers, and Ter Brugghen especially. The emotionally charged subject lends itself well to the rendering of the fine light-dark contrasts that these artists so loved. As the New Testament relates: 'And, behold, the Angel of the Lord come upon him, and a light shined in the prison' (Acts 12: 7). The contrast between the young angel with his cream-coloured skin and the old man with his weather-beaten face and hands is also exploited to great effect. These contrasts, together with the expressive body language and gestures, enhance the emotional impact of this painting.

After his apprenticeship, which he probably spent in Utrecht with Abraham Bloemaert (pp. 44-45), Hendrick ter Brugghen went to Italy, where he relates that he 'practised his art for a good many years'. It was in Rome that he became acquainted with the art of Caravaggio which is characterised by dramatic contrasts and naturalistic detail. Hendrick ter Brugghen is the most important exponent of the Utrecht school of Caravaggism, which flourished in the 1620s (cf. Gerard van Honthorst, pp. 90-91).

The deliverance of St Peter, 1624

Canvas, 105 x 85 cm

Inv. 966

The figures on this double portrait can be identified as Constantijn Huygens (1596-1687) and his wife Suzanna van Baerle (1599-1637), this painting being the only portrait of Suzanna to have been preserved. Huygens was secretary to three successive stadholders – Frederik Hendrik (p. 10, fig. 4), Willem II (1626-1650) and Willem III (1650-1702). As such he was at the heart of seventeenth-century political and cultural life and was portrayed on numerous occasions. Because of his great knowledge of the visual arts he played a major role in the formation of the stadholder's art collections, which includes the oldest nucleus of the present Mauritshuis collection (see Abraham Bloemaert, p. 44).

In the absence of Johan Maurits (p. 6, fig. 1), who spent several years in Brazil, Huygens oversaw the construction of the town palace designed by Van Campen that rose next to Huygens' home on the Plein – a building that has since been demolished (p. 10, fig. 5).

The music sheet held up by the two spouses illustrates the harmony in their marriage, which was a very happy one. Huygens, who became well-known as a musician and a poet, included loving descriptions of his wife under the pet name of 'Sterre' (Star) in many of his poems. The marriage came to an abrupt end with Suzanna's untimely death.

Double portraits are quite rare; it was more common in the seventeenth-century northern Netherlands for couples to be depicted separately. The composition is unusual because Suzanna looks at the viewer, whereas more traditional double portraits depicted both husband and wife in profile. This intriguing portrait can be dated around 1635.

In the same period Van Campen drew a portrait of Huygens's son, also named Constantijn (Haarlem, Teylers Museum). Van Campen, who is now known primarily as an architect, left a small oeuvre of paintings and drawings.

Jacob van Campen, 1596-1657

Portrait of Constantijn Huygens (1596-1687) and
Suzanna van Baerle (1599-1637), c.1635

Canvas, 95 x 78.5 cm
Inv. 1089
(permanent loan from the Friends
of the Mauritshuis Foundation, The Hague)

We are completely in the dark as to the life of Adriaen Coorte – even the years of his birth and death are unknown. His dated paintings tell us that he was active in the period 1683-1707, probably in Middelburg. Coorte specialised in still lifes and made more than hundred paintings. His compositions contain certain recurrent motifs: one is a stone plinth or table-top on which the artist places a single type of fruit or vegetable or a group of assorted shells, always set against a dark background.

This small painting, which – like many of Coorte's still lifes – was first painted on paper and subsequently pasted to a small board, is in many ways characteristic of the painter's compositions. Thus the hard but at the same time brilliantly elaborated lighting, which accents the strawberries and endows them with a near-magical quality, is typical of Coorte's paintings, as is the small size. It is striking that only the upper portion of the tabletop is illuminated, as a result of which the edge of the table stands out very sharply. The artist has depicted this simple array with great subtlety: the white flower makes a vertical element in the heaped-up fruits, while the playful way in which the two strawberries hang over the edge of the table add an element of liveliness. To the right of these two strawberries Coorte placed his signature and the year 1705. More than any other painter of still lifes he fashioned works of outstanding quality based on the most modest of subjects.

Adriaen Coorte, active *c.*1683-1707

Still life with strawberries, 1705
Paper on panel, 16.5 x 14 cm
Inv. 1106

When the States of Holland and West-Friesland decided, in 1660, to honour King Charles II (1630-1685) of England with a diplomatic gift, the object in question had to be chosen with care. Italian paintings were the favourite works of the sovereign, who was not particularly fond of 'modern masters'. Nonetheless, the choice for this 'Dutch Gift' included a work by Gerrit Dou, the Leiden *Feinmaler* who had been a pupil of Rembrandt. The king was so pleased with this painting, *The young mother*, that he tried to take Dou on as a court painter. Dou declined the honour, however, possibly mindful of a poem that warned those considering such a step: 'He who will curry favour with Kings must a slave and flatterer be'. The work also commanded the admiration of the English art critic John Evelyn (1620-1706), who referred to it as a 'Drolerie, or rather a Dutch Kitchin', lavishing especial praise on the enamel-like quality of the painting. Dou's masterpiece came to hang in Whitehall, as recalled by the inventory number '501' in the lower right corner.

When stadholder Willem III (1650-1702) became king of England, he brought *The young mother* back to the Netherlands, where it became part of the collection at Het Loo Palace. Later requests for its return were not heeded. In the collection of the House of Orange, Dou's painting served for many years as the companion-piece to Rembrandt's *Simeon's song of praise*, which was purchased in 1733 (pp. 110-111).

The young mother, 1658

Panel, 73.5 x 55.5 cm (rounded top)

Inv. 32

In 1626 Anthony van Dyck returned to Antwerp after a successful stay in Italy. He soon became the leading portrait artist of the burgher élite. In 1627 he was commissioned to make a portrait of the prosperous cloth merchant Peeter Stevens (1590-1668). Stevens was a man of some status, and as almoner he was responsible for the care of the poor, which involved substantial financial obligations. Besides enjoying the esteem due to this prestigious post, he was also admired for his large art collection. He collected works by famous old masters such as Jan van Eyck (c.1395-1441) and Pieter Bruegel the Elder (1520/25-1569).

On 12 March 1628, Stevens married Anna Wake (1605-before 1669), the daughter of a fabulously wealthy English merchant. For the occasion, her portrait was added to that of her husband. However, when Van Dyck had painted Stevens's likeness, he had not considered the possibility that the portrait might acquire a pendant. It is customary for the woman to be depicted on the right side of the man (from the viewer's point of view), which in this case would have meant placing Stevens with his back to his wife. As this was undesirable an exception was made, and Anna Wake was placed to the left of her husband.

To signify the marriage that had just been solemnised, Anna wears a wedding ring on her thumb. She is dressed in the very latest fashion, with a magnificent French-style collar, trimmed like the cuffs with Flemish bone lace. Also noteworthy are the puff sleeves: over white undersleeves she wears black strips of material bound together in the middle with a blue ribbon. The fan in her hand completes her smart outfit.

Anthony van Dyck, 1599-1641

Portrait of Peeter Stevens (1590-1668) and
Portrait of Anna Wake (1605-before 1669), 1627-1628

Canvas, each 112.5 x 99.5 cm
Inv. 239-240

This perhaps rather curious painting is both a history piece and a family portrait. The centre foreground is taken up by a bearded man in a rough habit holding up a lantern – the Greek philosopher Diogenes (fourth century BC), searching in broad daylight for an 'honest' man. The setting, a market-place in ancient Athens, has been transported here to Dutch surroundings – a prominent background feature is a church much resembling St Bavo's Church in Haarlem. At left we see a building spun by the painter's imagination, with classical columns and pilasters, that does not belong in Haarlem. Its entrance bears the date ('ANNO 1652') and the monogram ('CVE') of Caesar van Everdingen.

In the left background the Haarlem painter added another anecdote from the history of Diogenes. It shows a wheelbarrow of turnips being delivered, to serve as the philosopher's simple fare. He himself sits in a tub. In front of this 'cote dwelling' a man in a turban is leaning over towards him. This is Alexander the Great (356-323 BC), who promises to grant all his wishes. But the ascetic merely asks him to stop blocking the sunlight.

Caesar van Everdingen, *c.*1617-1678

Diogenes looking for an honest man, 1652

Canvas, 75.9 x 103.6 cm

Inv. 39

In 1654 Carel Fabritius depicted a small bird whose cleverness made it a very popular pet: a 'puttertje', as the goldfinch was called in the Netherlands. This nickname, which means 'water drawer', came from the bird's ability to draw water from a bowl using a smaller bowl – the size of a thimble – as a bucket. Old prints and paintings show how it was done. The gold-finch would let the small bowl down into a larger drinking bowl at the end of a cord, and then pull it back up brimming full.

Gerrit Dou, 1613-1675
Girl with bunch of grapes (detail), 1662
Panel, 38 x 29 cm
Turin, Galleria Sabauda

First it would have to raise the lid of the drinking bowl itself.

This panel may have been part of a goldfinch's cage, with the painted bird and the bowl serving as a *trompe-l'oeil*. A real bird-house would have been attached at the top, and a small shelf with a drinking bowl at the bottom. If this was indeed the case, it is understandable why the signature and date were added so conspicuously.

Carel Fabritius was apprenticed to Rembrandt in Amsterdam around 1641-1643. His oeuvre is small – no more than about a dozen paintings. These are characterised by loose brushstrokes, a varied palette and a subtle handling of light. In 1654, the year in which Fabritius painted the goldfinch, he died in the explosion of the powder magazine in Delft. Johannes Vermeer (pp. 144-147), who also worked in Delft, may have been influenced by Fabritius's handling of light.

The goldfinch, 1654

Panel, 33.5 x 22.8 cm
Inv. 605

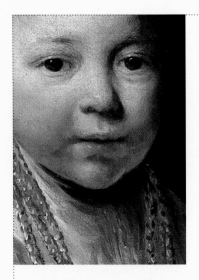

precious stone at the end. This was partly for her to bite on, but it also served as a charm to ward off disease and accident at a time when child mortality was extremely high. She carries a straw basket with raisins or other dried fruit, and may be holding a fig. She is leaning against a high-chair, the door of which (through which a chamber pot could be inserted) is open. A few pieces of chalk are strewn on the chair.

This unknown little girl is dressed in a white smock with long skirts, a garment much favoured by girls and women in the 1630s and 1640s. She also wears an apron, and on her head she has a tight-fitting bonnet with a garland of flowers and a green veil. Children often wore white in this period – this colour tended to be associated with youth. The garland seems to have been spun from the painter's imagination, however, as it was no part of everyday clothing. The little child has a cord with a rattle and a semi-

Whereas the background and chair are painted in wide, Rembrandtesque strokes, the child's face is executed with extreme delicacy, enhanced by carefully placed accents in blue and grey. Govert Flinck would gradually change his style of painting in the 1640s. In Rembrandt's studio he had learnt to paint in brown hues and clearly visible brushstrokes, but he gradually opted instead for a smoother manner of painting, elegant compositions and bright colours, all of which was more fashionable.

Govert Flinck, 1615-1660

Girl by a high-chair, 1640

Canvas, 114.3 x 87.1 cm
Inv. 676

Arent de Gelder trained with Rembrandt around 1662, making him the master's last pupil. His apprenticeship greatly influenced his style, which is characterised by wide brushstrokes, dark colours and strong highlights. It is striking that the Dordrecht master continued to work in this fashion well into the eighteenth century, when all around him the vogue was for *Feinmalerei* and a light-coloured palette. De Gelder's financial independence will doubtless have made it easier for him to follow his chosen path. A preference for biblical scenes was something else he shared with Rembrandt. The painting discussed here shows the story of Simeon, who bursts into song when he sees the Infant Jesus and recognises in Him the Messiah, a subject that Rembrandt too depicted several times (pp. 110-111).

However strong Rembrandt's influence may have been, De Gelder was certainly no mere imitator of his illustrious teacher. He used thinner, more fluid paint, for instance, in which he scratched away to his heart's content. It is above all his application of paint and colour that makes De Gelder such an interesting artist. *Simeon's song of praise* – one of his best works – is a fine example of his style. De Gelder used green, grey and cream in an astonishing range of hues, which is exemplified in the Christ Child's swaddling clothes. Accents have been added in red, orange, yellow and white. The artist scratched and scraped away paint while it was still wet to reveal the layer beneath. In Mary's striped shawl he actually seems to have done this with his finger.

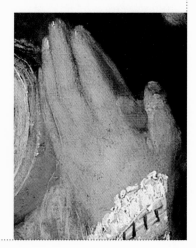

Arent de Gelder, 1645-1727

*Simeon's song of praise, c.*1700

Canvas, 94.5 x 107.5 cm
Inv. 1047
(permanent loan from the Friends
of the Mauritshuis Foundation, The Hague)

Floris van Egmond (1469-1539), Count of Buren and Leerdam and Lord of IJsselstein, was a high-ranking officer who fought in both the Burgundian and Hapsburg armies. This formidable war-horse rose to the rank of captain general in the army of Emperor Charles V (1500-1558). In 1518 Floris became Stadholder of Holland, Zeeland and West Friesland. Van Egmond was a close friend of Philip of Burgundy (1464-1524), who had become bishop of Utrecht in 1517. Philip had an aversion to administrative matters, preferring to divide his time between science and art like a true Renaissance ruler. As the bishop's court painter, Jan Gossaert made a great many portraits of his friends and family.

Gossaert depicted Van Egmond not as a soldier but as a noble-man. A striking detail of his clothing is the pinkish-red jerkin with slits revealing a layer of gold brocade. Over this he wears a gown of fine white damask and a collar of brown fur, possibly sable. From his neck dangles the jewel of the order of the Golden Fleece, identifiable by its ram's fleece, flint and fire steel. Membership of this prestigious chivalric order was reserved for the most eminent of nobles. Gossaert's rendering of the jewel provides additional information, as the attributes hang from a velvet ribbon rather than a chain. This was not allowed until 1516, which means that the painting cannot have been produced before that year. The 'L' at right in the painting is not the artist's monogram (as has sometimes been assumed) but a Roman numeral representing Van Egmond's age in 1519. The painting was therefore probably made in that year.

74

Jan Gossaert, 1478-1532

*Portrait of Floris van Egmond (1469-1539), c.*1519

Panel, 39.8 x 29.3 cm

Inv. 841

(long-term loan from the Rijksmuseum, Amsterdam)

Jan van Goyen was among the first generation of painters to apply himself exclusively to rendering the Dutch landscape. He was unequalled in his ability to convey the atmosphere of the watery Dutch scenery. Van Goyen worked at high speed and was immensely productive as a result: more than 1,200 paintings by him have been preserved.

This panel from his mature, late period shows a river landscape with the view of a village dominated by its church tower rising up above the houses. Although no existing location is depicted here, the church tower displays similarities to that of Ouderkerk on the river Amstel. In the foreground we glimpse the opposite bank, where a ferry rowing-boat has just moored under the watchful eyes of a dog. This motif, which is painted in dark hues, enforces the depth in the composition. Where the river bends to the left in the background, a windmill and a few farmhouses are ranged along the horizon, with clearly perceptible brushstrokes painted wet-in-wet. The panel

has been laid in with rapid, sure strokes in a limited palette of beige and brown tints. In the dark portions, Van Goyen has used the dark ground layer beneath, which glimmers through in places.

It was around 1629-1630 that Van Goyen started to develop the prototype of the river landscape with a sloping bank, a motif that was also much used by Salomon van Ruysdael (1600/3-1670) and to which he returns here. Around the same time he reduced his palette to a few earth colours. This predominantly monochrome quality was to be a constant factor in his paintings.

Jan van Goyen, 1596-1656

River scene with church and farmhouse, 1653

Panel, 27.5 x 42 cm
Inv. 1100

At first sight this is nothing but an interior with paintings, of which untold examples are known by Flemish masters such as Jan Brueghel the Elder (1568-1625) and David Teniers the Younger (1610-1690). On closer inspection, however, this picture proves to be far more complex. Willem van Haecht made this art collection into a history piece, and ultimately even into a tribute to seventeenth-century Flemish painting.

Van Haecht's known oeuvre comprises only about four paintings, all of art collections, and a modest number of prints. Besides being a painter Van Haecht was also the keeper of the art collection of Cornelis van der Geest (1555-1638), a patron of the arts in Antwerp. Van der Geest's paintings loom large in the work of Van Haecht, as exemplified here. The impressive *Battle of the Amazons* (Munich, Alte Pinakothek), for instance, which hangs above the table, was painted by Peter Paul Rubens (pp. 122-123) for Van der Geest around 1615.

Depicted at lower left is the tale of Apelles and Campaspe. Apelles was court painter of Alexander the Great (356-323 BC). In the version related by Pliny the Elder (*Naturalis Historia*), Apelles fell in love with Campaspe, Alexander's most beautiful concubine, after he had been hired to make a portrait of her. When Alexander noticed this he generously gave Campaspe to Apelles. He himself was content to possess the painting, which was so lifelike! This gesture to an artist on the part of a ruler was a much loved *topos* among artists.

The small group at lower left is surrounded by paintings from Antwerp: beside Campaspe is a hunting scene by Jan Brueghel the Elder and Rubens, next to that a market scene by Joachim Beuckelaer (*c.*1533/4-*c.*1574) and a flower still life by Daniel Seghers (1590-1661), and at the far right is *The money-changer and his wife* by Quinten Massys (*c.*1465-1530), now in the Musée du Louvre in Paris.

Willem van Haecht, 1593-1637

Apelles painting Campaspe, c.1630?

Panel, 104.9 x 148.7 cm
Inv. 266

This laughing boy is rendered with a striking characterisation and infectiously disarming quality that are unique to Frans Hals. The boy unabashedly exposes his brown teeth, and his tangled hair has not seen a comb for a long time. His face radiates good cheer. This virtuoso portrait exemplifies the free brushstrokes which earned Hals such renown. We clearly see the rapid movements of the brush with which the face and collar were painted. The painting may be described as the study of a face – in any case it is far from a true portrait.

It would seem that Frans Hals, who produced almost nothing but portraits, used studies of this kind in particular to experiment in a rough technique. In commissioned portraits he adopted a more precise, if not exactly smooth, style of painting. As the artist grew older – and more experienced – he increasingly applied the rough style in portraits too. The painter Karel van Mander (1548-1606), who was Hals's teacher, writes

of the coexistence of the 'smooth' and the 'rough' manner, and believed that the rough manner was the prerogative of great masters. Although portrait painting as such was thought to be beneath the dignity of great artists, Hals was celebrated by his contemporaries.

Frans Hals, 1581/5-1666

Laughing boy, c.1627

Panel, diameter 29.5 cm
Inv. 1032

Jan Davidsz de Heem is one of the most important and most versatile still life painters of the seventeenth century. From about 1630 onwards he worked in Antwerp, where he largely specialised in still-life displays. In or around 1650 he started applying himself to flower pieces, probably inspired by the work of the Antwerp Jesuit Daniel Seghers (1590-1661). He was responsible for a number of innovations, the most important of which being the seemingly loose, casual manner in which the bouquet overlaps the rim of the vase, filling the entire pictorial surface. He also revived the colourful palette that had been so characteristic of Flemish flower pieces in the day of Jan Brueghel the Elder (1568-1625).

The flower piece discussed here was probably made around 1670, when the artist was still living and working in Utrecht, the city of his birth. It is in extremely good condition, partly because it was never relined, which is exceptional for a seventeenth-century canvas. De Heem's marvellous technique is visible in details such as the hairy caterpillars and fragile butterflies, the broken ears of corn and the stems in the transparent vase. The glass vase reflects the window of the artist's studio, complete with cloudy skies.

As De Heem lived alternately in the southern and northern Netherlands, he acted as a connecting link between the somewhat sober still lifes of the north and the more exuberant ones of the south. His output was immense, but fewer than twenty flower still lifes by his hand are known today.

Jan Davidsz de Heem, 1606-1683/4

Vase with flowers, c.1670

Canvas, 74.2 x 52.6 cm
Inv. 1099
(permanent loan from the Friends
of the Mauritshuis Foundation, The Hague)

The Oudezijds Voorburgwal, which links the river Amstel in the south to the IJ in the north, is the oldest city canal in Amsterdam. For his painting Jan van der Heyden chose one of the most appealing stretches, near the Bierkaai and the Oude Kerk (Old Church). Along the Bierkaai, or 'Beer wharf', the beer – foreign beer in this case – was unloaded in barrels. The dominant Oude Kerk was built in the fourteenth and fifteenth centuries, making it the oldest Gothic hall church in the northern Netherlands. In 1658 and 1659 the chimes, which are clearly visible in the painting, were completely renewed.

Although this city scene was painted after life, Van der Heyden took a few liberties with his subject. The clock tower is in reality taller and slimmer, and the canal is also somewhat narrower. The meticulous attention to detail, allowing us to distinguish each individual brick of the façade, is typical of this artist. The many figures that enliven the city scene are probably by Adriaen van de Velde (1636-1672), who was usually hired for this work by Van der Heyden.

City scenes and landscapes with country homes were Jan van der Heyden's speciality. But he was an inventor as well as an artist. In 1668 he devised an ingenious plan for Amsterdam's city lights, which would continue to be used until 1840. In 1672 he constructed a pump and hose device for fighting fires, which actually went into production in 1681.

Jan van der Heyden, 1637-1712

View of the Oudezijds Voorburgwal with the Bierkaai
and the Oude Kerk in Amsterdam, c.1670?

Panel, 41.2 x 52.5 cm
Inv. 868

For many years Meindert Hobbema was overshadowed by his teacher, Jacob van Ruisdael (pp. 124-125). But at the beginning of the nineteenth century he was rediscovered and his works vanished abroad for huge sums of money. The sole remaining monumental painting by him in a Dutch public collection (the Mauritshuis) was donated to the Canadian people in 1950 in gratitude for their part in liberating the Netherlands in 1944-1945. With the acquisition in 1994 of this *Wooded landscape with cottages*, however, it is once again possible to view one of the master's monumental paintings in the Netherlands. The painting was produced around 1665 in Hobbema's best period, and is regarded as one of his finest works.

Although strongly influenced by Van Ruisdael, Hobbema's landscapes are less overwhelming and dramatic. This wooded landscape has instead an open composition and the use of light could even be called playful. Features characteristic of Hobbema include the sun-drenched apertures through which we glimpse the background, adding much to the picture's liveliness and depth. This effect is enhanced by the varied palette. The trees on the right, for instance, are rendered in dozens of shades of green and brown.

Hobbema had a limited store of motifs - the same copses, windmills and farms turn up in his work with great regularity. But it is a mark of his great talent that he was always able to combine these elements into surprising new compositions. This, together with his unerring loose brushstrokes and superb sense of colour, has yielded magnificent results that are among the highlights of Dutch landscape painting.

Meindert Hobbema, 1638-1709

Wooded landscape with cottages, c.1665

Canvas, 88 x 120.7 cm

Inv. 1105

Hans Holbein the Younger, 1497/8-1543
Portrait of a 28-year old falconer, 1542
Panel, 25 x 19 cm
The Hague, Mauritshuis

The inscription on this portrait of a nobleman with a falcon gives his name and age in Latin: he is Robert Cheseman and his portrait was made in 1533 when he was 48 years of age. This is beyond dispute a masterpiece by Hans Holbein the Younger. Soon after he settled in England in 1532, the painter from southern Germany made a great name for himself with his extremely lively portraits of affluent merchants in London and prominent courtiers, each one executed in minute detail. Four years later he became court painter to Henry VIII (1491-1547). Robert Cheseman (1485-1547), Lord of Southall and Norwood, was a powerful and wealthy man, who held numerous public offices. He regularly accompanied Henry VIII on hunting parties, and is depicted in his position of the king's Grand Falconer.

Cheseman is dressed in the fashion of his times. He wears his hair well down over his ears and is clean-shaven. A royal decree of May 1535 laid down that mature men at court should thenceforth grow beards and cut their hair short, as illustrated by another portrait by Hans Holbein, dated 1542, also in the Mauritshuis. It shows an unknown nobleman with a hawk on his hand. Both portraits of courtiers with hunting birds belonged to the English royal house for a long time, until Stadholder Willem III (1650-1702) took them to Het Loo Palace at the end of the seventeenth century. After his death, Queen Anne (1665-1714) made an unsuccessful attempt to claim them as the property of the crown. Since 1822 they have been among the showpieces of the Mauritshuis.

Hans Holbein the Younger, 1497/8-1543

Portrait of Robert Cheseman (1485-1547), 1533

Panel, 58.8 x 62.8 cm

Inv. 276

This feathered fiddler grins at us provocatively. Her daring costume, the bright colours and the strong play of light all enhance the frivolity of the image. Gerard van Honthorst of Utrecht painted this courtesan in 1626. Six years earlier he had returned from Italy, where, like his fellow townsman Hendrick ter Brugghen (pp. 56-57), he had undergone the influence of the art of Caravaggio (1571-1610), with its characteristically dramatic light-dark contrasts. His nocturnal pieces earned Van Honthorst the name in Italy of 'Gherardo delle notti'. But while Ter Brugghen had adopted Caravaggio's unpolished naturalism, Van Honthorst's paintings have a more idealised quality. His somewhat smoother style appealed to courtly circles at home and abroad, where he was greatly in demand as a portraitist and history painter.

In the 1620s Van Honthorst painted countless musicians as half-figures, a popular theme derived from the repertoire of Caravaggio and his Italian followers. It is not only the sitter's saucy clothing and coquettish smile that produce the erotic undertone of *The violin player*. The violin was not considered altogether respectable at the time because of its erotic connotations. The musician leans the instrument against her shoulder rather than her chin, in accordance with seventeenth-century custom, and uses the 'French grasp', placing her thumb under the hair of the bow. This was a common grasp when playing popular dance music, which would appear to suit the occasion here.

Gerard van Honthorst, 1590-1656

The violin player, 1626

Canvas, 84.5 x 66 cm
Inv. 1107

Three years after the conclusion of the Treaty of Münster in 1648, which marked the end of the Eighty Years' War, the Netherlands' war of independence, Houckgeest painted this attractive interior of the Nieuwe Kerk in Delft. At the centre is the mausoleum, designed by Hendrick de Keyser (1565-1621), of Willem I (1533-1584) – known in the Netherlands as Willem the Silent, 'Father of the Fatherland' – who had been assassinated in Delft in 1584. To the people of the newly independent Republic, this monument must have possessed enormous emotional and symbolic significance. This is undoubtedly why Houckgeest chose to depict this particular side of the tomb, with the statue representing Liberty. He uses the couple with the child looking up at the statue to ensure that the viewer's attention is also drawn to it.

Houckgeest produced only a small oeuvre, but he played an important role in the development of the northern Netherlandish church interior. In or around 1650 he innovated the genre by chosing a diagonal perspective, depicting only a corner of the church. In this respect he clearly distinguished himself from the other great painter of church interiors, Pieter Saenredam (pp. 126-127). One of the most attractive aspects of Houckgeest's church interiors is his attention to detail. Examples here include the memorial plaques for members of the Orange family on the choir walls and the graffiti on the column in the foreground.

The tomb of Willem of Orange in Delft, 1651

Panel, 56 x 38 cm

Inv. 58

In the gospel according to St Luke, shepherds in the fields are visited by angels who tell them of the birth of Jesus. They go to Bethlehem, where they find Mary, Joseph and the Christ Child in a stable. The three angel's heads at upper left in this picture refer to the heavenly tidings in the fields, but the rest of the painting is taken up with the adoration of the shepherds in the stable.

Jacob Jordaens painted this scene in about 1617, at the very beginning of his long career. The influence of the Italian painter Caravaggio (1571-1610) is clearly visible in the strong contrast between light and dark areas and the realism with which the figures are depicted. The furrowed head of Joseph and the old woman at the back are splendid examples of this.

The strength of the composition is greatly enhanced by the fact that most of the figures are cut off by the edge of the picture – another invention of Caravaggio's. The light comes from a source outside and to the left of the image. The way the light falls on the copper jug at lower left is highly suggestive. Jordaens must have been very pleased with this painting, as in 1618 and 1619 he made two virtually identical versions, which are now in The Metropolitan Museum of Art in New York and the Nationalmuseum in Stockholm.

Jordaens enrolled as a painter in the St Luke's Guild of Antwerp in 1615. He regularly worked with Peter Paul Rubens and Anthony van Dyck. After Rubens's death in 1640 he took over the latter's role in executing monumental commissions.

Jacob Jordaens, 1593-1678

The adoration of the shepherds, c.1617

Panel, 125.5 x 96 cm

Inv. 937

With a keen eye for authentic detail, Hans Memling has portrayed this man at prayer from close by. The man is set against a panoramic vista that may be Flemish, judging by the village church and the step-gabled house in the left background. His attire includes a jerkin lined with costly lynx fur and a cruciform piece of jewellery decorated with pearls. With his dark curls and scarred nose, the subject has a striking appearance.

The back of this panel is painted with the man's family coat of arms – the armorial bearings were later painted over by another hand. The underlying, original arms can be identified as those of the Lespinette family (De l'Espinette or De Lépinette) from Franche-Comté. Which scion of this family had his likeness immortalised in the late fifteenth century by the renowned painter from Bruges has not yet been ascertained.

Both the painted back of this panel and the pose – the man is facing left in prayer – indicate that this piece was not originally made as an independent portrait. In all probability it was part of a diptych whose left panel depicted the Virgin and Child, to whom the sitter was addressing his prayer, as it were – this companion-piece has been lost. Dendrochronological analysis of the panel narrows down the date of this portrait to the period 1485-1490.

Reverse of the panel

Hans Memling, 1435/40-1491

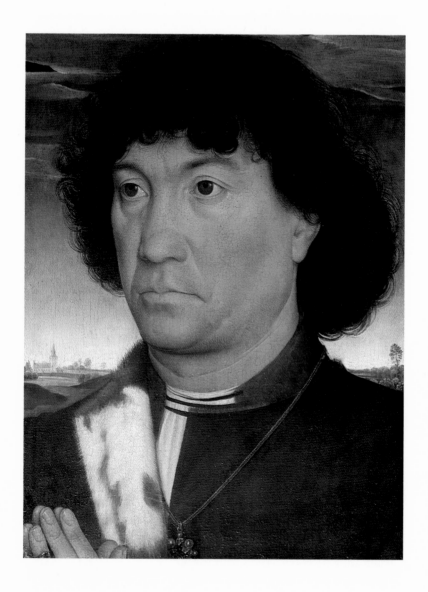

Portrait of a man from the Lespinette family, c.1485-1490

Panel, 30.1 x 22.3 cm

Inv. 595

This serene picture is one of the high points in the mature work of the Leiden-born painter Gabriel Metsu, who did not start working in the meticulous manner of the Leiden *Feinmaler* until after his move to Amsterdam. In this exquisite scene, which may be dated around 1662-1663, the viewer's glance is drawn automatically to the shimmering materials of the clothing, which are painted masterfully in invisible brushstrokes.

Around the same time, one of the most imposing edifices in the northern Netherlands had been built at Dam Square in Amsterdam – the town hall (now the Royal Palace) designed by Jacob van Campen (p. 58). For the fireplace in the background, with rich and fashionable decorations suggestive of a prosperous household, Metsu based himself on the monumental example in the burgomaster's room in the town hall. The painting of a ship in the stormy seas, however, was born of his own imagination and contrasts with the subdued and harmonious scene.

The painter appears to have added this detail as a warning about the fickleness of love, compared by some seventeenth-century writers and poets with a ship at sea. The lady seated at the table is rapt in concentration writing the text or notes for a song (a love song?) that she would sing to the accompaniment of a lute. This instrument, which is being played by the figure on the left, is traditionally associated with harmony, especially within marriage. Even so, it is not very likely that the allusion here is to a marriage between the writing lady and the gentleman behind her, of whose presence she is quite unaware.

Gabriel Metsu, 1629-1667

A young woman composing music, c.1662-1663

Panel, 57.5 x 43.5 cm

Inv. 94

In this marvellously painted picture, Frans van Mieris has given a subtle rendering of a scene in a brothel. It is only when we look more closely that we see that the soldier with his striking red cloak is tugging at the apron of the maidservant with her low *décolletage*, suggesting that something is going on between them. The little dogs mating behind the soldier, the male of which was once painted out, are an unequivocal detail in this picture. The man of the couple in the background is recognisable as the painter himself.

Van Mieris's paintings are characterised by refined, invisible brushstrokes and the liveliness of the diminutive scenes. Here too, it is the style of painting as much as the subject-matter that appeals to the imagination. The rendering of the various materials and surfaces almost defies belief: witness the shiny fabric of the maidservant's clothes and the sublimely painted reflection on the pewter flagon and the soldier's metal cuirass.

Van Mieris and his teacher Gerrit Dou (p. 62) are the prime exponents of the Leiden school of *Feinmalerei*. This painting stems from the early period of Van Mieris, who produced a series of masterpieces within a brief space of time, of a quality he did not equal later on.

Frans van Mieris the Elder, 1635-1681

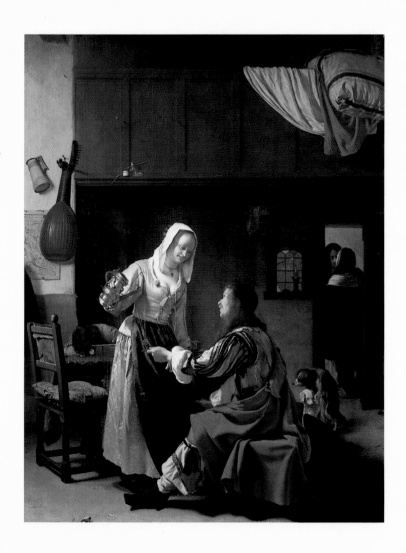

Brothel scene, c.1658

Panel, 42.8 x 33.3 cm
Inv. 860

Three men sit around a small table in a rather messy interior: one is lighting his long, clay pipe from the glowing coals in the coal pan, while his companion facing him, who has a jug in his left hand and wears an apron, raises his glass in a toast, and the third tunes his fiddle. In the semi-circular opening leading out into a courtyard sits a girl who is teasing a little dog with a bone. A woman (the innkeeper's wife?) is pulling up another chair and three men are talking by the fireside in the background. At left a flight of stairs leads upstairs. Pots and pans and other household goods are arrayed on the walls. This peaceful scene from the lives of ordinary people is signed and dated 1662.

Adriaen van Ostade continued a tradition in peasant scenes that goes back to Pieter Bruegel the Elder (1520/25-1569) and his followers. In the seventeenth century, paintings of this kind, in which the peasantry is sometimes portrayed as excessively dim-witted or coarse, were dubbed 'grillen'

or 'grollitjes' (caprices, antics). Adriaen Brouwer (p. 52) was a major exponent of this genre. Likewise Adriaen van Ostade, at least until around 1640. After this his outlook became milder and more poetic. Moreover, his palette, which had been fairly mono-chrome at the beginning of his career, gradually became warmer. His best works date from the 1650s and 1660s. The piece shown here, which displays an extremely subtle use of light and in which the bright red and blue colours of the figures' clothes are set against a more monochrome background, is one of the most splendid examples from this period.

Adriaen van Ostade, 1610-1685

Peasants in an inn, 1662

Panel, 47.5 x 39 cm

Inv. 128

The Haarlem artist Isack van Ostade produced a substantial oeuvre of paintings and drawings in the space of about ten years, before dying at an early age. Like his elder brother and teacher Adriaen van Ostade (p. 50), Isack specialised in peasant scenes, generally with an outdoor setting. Aside from his brother's influence, Italianate art with its sun-drenched landscapes clearly played an important role in Isack's development. He evolved a style of his own, characterised by subtle hues and a refined use of light and shade effects. Van Ostade's landscapes consist primarily of winter landscapes and scenes outside farmhouses or inns. This painting, from 1645, is one of the finest examples of the latter.

Van Ostade's paintings tend to be similar in composition. The image is divided in two by a diagonal (in this case a country road) while there is a suggestion of the continuation of the scene into the distance, with the buildings and figures depicted on the right and the horizon on the left. Here a motley assembly has gathered outside a ramshackle country inn. An anomalous element among the crowds of simple working people is a richly dressed lady on a peasant's cart. A beggar raises his hat to her, while a cripple approaches her with his little dog. In the accurately observed rendering of the different horses, dogs, chickens and the long-haired pig in the foreground, Van Ostade also proves himself a gifted animal painter. A regular eye-catcher in his pictures is the grey horse, which in this case is scratching its leg in an extremely lifelike way. Despite the many anecdotal details, Van Ostade succeeds in creating unity in his image through a combination of a clear composition with a subtle use of colours.

Isack van Ostade, 1621-1649

Travellers outside an inn, 1645

Panel, 75 x 109 cm

Inv. 789

On 25 October 1636 Johan Maurits of Nassau-Siegen (p. 6, fig. 1) – founder of the Mauritshuis – left for Brazil, where the West India Company had appointed him governor-general. His retinue included scientists and artists, among whom was the painter Frans Post. Post's years in Brazil left such a deep impression on him that he devoted himself almost exclusively to Brazilian landscapes for the rest of his life.

At present seven of the paintings Post produced in Brazil are known, the *View of the island of Itamaraca* being the earliest. Itamaraca lies about thirty kilometres northeast of the city of Recife. This view shows the stretch of the island that faces Rio Iguarassu, with Fort Orange and a few houses in the small town of Schoppe just visible at the far right. The composition of this picture is characteristic of the landscapes Post made in Brazil. The horizon is low, the landscape makes a flat impression and water takes up much of the view. Only a few human figures populate what is for the rest a largely empty landscape, but they fulfil an essential role. Three of the four figures are seen from behind, which intensifies the picture's air of barrenness.

In 1679 Johan Maurits presented a large number of paintings to King Louis XIV (1638-1715) of France. They included at least six of the paintings Frans Post produced in Brazil, among others this *View of the island of Itamaraca*. Four are still in Paris today, in the Musée du Louvre.

Frans Post, *c.*1612-1680

View of the island of Itamaraca, 1637

Canvas, 63.5 x 88.5 cm
Inv. 915
(long-term loan from the Rijksmuseum, Amsterdam)

Nowadays most visitors to the Mauritshuis come primarily to see the paintings by Rembrandt, Johannes Vermeer, Jan Steen and Frans Hals. But for much of the eighteenth and nineteenth centuries it was the fame of 'Potter's bull' that drew crowds from far and wide. The combination of this subject, the life-sized format and the astonishing realism of this painting – including details such as the flies on the bull's coat and the cow's 'damp' nose – make it the epitome of Dutch painting.

Until a few years ago, it was generally assumed that Potter had depicted an existing bull. This is not the case, how-ever – the wide discrepancies between the different parts of the body rule it out. The drooping dewlap and horns are indicative of a two-year-old animal. The teeth, however, six of which are permanent ones, are those of a bull aged three or four. The forequarters are highly muscular, whereas the hindquarters are rather undeveloped. The perspective is also slightly askew. The fore- and hind-quarters are at an angle to the pictorial plane, whereas the middle of the animal's body is parallel to it. The only possible conclusion is that Potter composed the bull from a number of preliminary studies of different animals.

Potter's oeuvre mostly consists of small cabinet pieces. The first design for *The bull* was not of its present size. Seams in the canvas that are still visible indicate that Potter initially intended to paint only the bull. At a later stage he attached linen strips on either side and along the top, on which he added the other animals, the farmer and the landscape.

Paulus Potter, 1625-1654

The bull, 1647

Canvas, 235.5 x 339 cm
Inv. 136

All the paintings acquired directly from Rembrandt in the collections of the House of Orange passed into foreign ownership in the course of the seventeenth century. It was not until 1733 that Willem Karel Hendrik Friso (1711-1751, the later Stadholder Willem IV) purchased another work by the most important painter of the Golden Age: *Simeon's song of praise*, described in the auction catalogue as 'Painted in a meticulous and detailed manner (and) from his best period'.

It was hung at Het Loo Palace as a companion-piece to Gerrit Dou's *Young mother* (pp. 62-63), which had been added to the stadholder's collection around 1700. This painting was about the same size, but semi-circular at the top. So the top left and right corners of Rembrandt's panel were sawn off and an extra sickle-shaped piece of panel added instead. The two paintings were also given identical gilt frames. Today, Rembrandt's painting once again appears in its original format in a rectangular frame, though the mutilations in the upper corners remain visible.

Rembrandt was particularly fond of the biblical tale of the pious Simeon, who sees the infant Jesus in the temple and recognises him as the Saviour (Luke 2: 25-33). He depicted the theme in numerous paintings, drawings and etchings. This panel, which is dated 1631, concludes Rembrandt's Leiden period and recapitulates all his artistic skills at that time. The carefully considered composition and multiplicity of details recall his teacher, Pieter Lastman (1583-1633), but both are subordinate to the concentrated, dramatic play of light on the protagonists, which is Rembrandt's most powerful vehicle of expression. All attention focuses on Simeon and the Christ Child, with Mary kneeling at their side.

Simeon's song of praise, 1631

Panel, 60.9 x 47.8 cm (rounded upper edges)

Inv. 145

In 1632 Rembrandt put the final touches to the most important commission he had been granted thus far – the painting of an anatomical demonstration by the 'praelector' or chief surgeon of the Amsterdam surgeons' guild, Dr Nicolaes Tulp. It was partly to execute this commission that Rembrandt left his birthplace Leiden for good. Three group portraits hung at the weighing-house where the guild met to view the annual anatomical demonstration, recording similar events in the past. Rembrandt saw these pieces, which dated from 1603, 1619 and 1625 respectively, and realised that his artistic freedom would be subject to constraints. The portraits of all participants had to be rendered clearly, with the protagonist, Dr Tulp, being accorded pride of place.

Tulp virtually fills the entire right half of the canvas, and with his black hat he dominates the scene. The surgeon depicted at the back, Frans van Loenen, also wore a hat to begin with, but Rembrandt later painted it out. Jacob Colevelt joined the group portrait at the last minute, and was added on the left. The names of the gentlemen were added later (not by Rembrandt) to the paper held by the surgeon Hartman Hartmansz. Not listed, however, is the name of the cadaver – Aris Kindt, a multiple offender whose body was handed over to the medical guild to be used for research after he was hanged in 1632.

In Rembrandt's hands, this group portrait became more than a stately row of fashionable poseurs. The composition has a dynamic quality and there is tremendous symbolism in the three hands at the centre: that of the dead man, the operating right hand of Dr Tulp and his demonstrating left hand. The surgeons' attention is fixed on this magical triangle and to the lesson Tulp is teaching: 'Know thyself'.

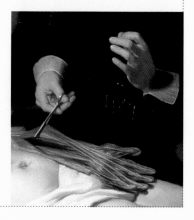

Rembrandt, 1606-1669

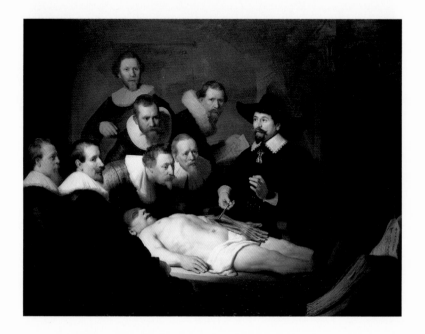

The anatomy lesson of Dr Nicolaes Tulp, 1632

Canvas, 169.5 x 216.5 cm

Inv. 146

The Old Testament relates that Suzanna was a Godfearing woman with a rich husband. Two elders, both judges, concealed themselves in her garden one day to spy on her while she was bathing. Threatening to spread slanderous rumours about her, they tried to seduce her, but Suzanna repulsed their advances (Daniel 13: 19-23). Of the two men hidden away in the shrubbery, Rembrandt shows only the face of one and a fragment of the other's turban. Suzanna does not see her assailants, but listens in horror to their indecent proposal. She protects her breast with her left hand while shielding her genitals with the other, expressing a mix of diffidence and revulsion. These gestures have a long history as representations of women's shame.

Rembrandt had a direct example for this work, in the painting of the same subject by his former teacher Pieter Lastman (1583-1633) which he copied in a drawing. Lastman had painted the elders full-length, and showed Suzanna making a rather vague gesture of protest. In his copy, Rembrandt drew her expression the way he would later paint it: he transformed Lastman's play into a dramatic one-act performance with Suzanna's nudity as its theme.

Suzanna, 1636

Panel, 47.4 x 38.6 cm
Inv. 147

Rembrandt, 1606-1669
Homer dictating to a scribe, c.1660
Pen and brush, 14.5 x 16.7 cm
Stockholm, Nationalmuseum

In most cases we are ignorant
of who commissioned
Rembrandt's paintings; *Homer,*
like *The anatomy lesson of
Dr Nicolaes Tulp,* is one of
the very few exceptions.
Together with two other
historical portraits, it was
painted for one of Rembrandt's
Italian patrons, the Sicilian
nobleman Don Antonio
Ruffo (1610-1678). Ruffo had
purchased *Aristotle with the
bust of Homer* (New York,
The Metropolitan Museum
of Art) from Rembrandt in
1653, and later he also ordered
a likeness of Alexander the
Great. Rembrandt had drawn
Homer declaiming poetry
in 1652 as a contribution to
the friendship album of Jan
Six (1618-1700). Six may
have suggested combining
these classical heroes into
a triptych, as it were, with
Homer (*c.*800-750 BC)
personifying poetry, Aristotle
(384-322 BC) philosophy
and Alexander (356-323 BC)
the active life. In his portrait
of the Greek poet and the
rendering of his bust in
the portrait of Aristotle,
Rembrandt based himself
on a copy after a late
Hellenistic sculpture, which
was part of his art collection.

Ruffo's paintings were
split up in the eighteenth
century, and *Homer* was
badly damaged in a fire.
The blind poet raises his
hand in a rhetorical gesture
and dictates his verses to
a scribe who has been
obliterated. The scribe's
paper, two fingers clasping
a pen and the neck of an
inkpot are still visible in
the lower right corner.
A drawing by Rembrandt
that may have been intended
as a design for the image
includes a depiction of
the rapt disciple of Homer
on the right. This means
the painting must have
originally been much wider,
corresponding to the scene
that was painted around
1700 by Rembrandt's pupil
Arent de Gelder (p. 72).

116

Rembrandt, 1606-1669

Homer, 1663

Canvas, 107 x 82 cm
Inv. 584

Rembrandt painted this moving portrait of an elderly man in 1667, almost at the end of his career. Nothing about it, however, points to the painter's advanced age – quite the contrary. The powerful and at the same time almost playful manner in which the paint has been applied, demonstrates that in his final years as a painter Rembrandt had reached the very peak of his mature powers. This portrait is a dazzling display of his skill. In the thinly painted dark clothing Rembrandt has made scratches in the wet paint at several points, revealing the golden-ochre layer beneath. The paint of the head, hands, collar and cuffs, on the other hand, has been applied with an impasto technique, largely wet-in-wet. The white collar and the cuffs make superb accents in the dark image. The man's face is made up of numerous small areas of paint, which Rembrandt has modelled using not only his brush but also his palette knife and the back of the brush. It is as if he fashioned the head in one continuous process, and wanted viewers to watch his 'work in progress'. This method is characteristic of Rembrandt's style in his final years.

The almost ruthless honesty with which Rembrandt has portrayed this man, whose identity is yet unknown, makes an indelible impression. Slumped in a chair somewhat, collar unfastened and hat askew, he seems almost oblivious to the fact that the painter is observing him. The combination of this acute observation, the brilliant painting technique, the work's incredibly good condition and the fact that no Dutch collection possessed a similar piece, made the museum decide to purchase this painting from a private collection in England.

Rembrandt, 1606-1669

Portrait of an elderly man, 1667

Canvas, 81.9 x 67.7 cm
Inv. 1118

This is the last self-portrait by Rembrandt. The painter signed and dated it at left centre: 'Rembrandt f[ecit= made it] 1669'. The supreme master of the Golden Age of Dutch painting died on 4 October 1669, at 63 years of age. It was an age attained by few of his contemporaries. His first wife, Saskia van Uylenburgh (1612-1642), was only 29 when she died in 1642. His second great love, Hendrickje Stoffels (1626-1663), died in 1663 at 37 years of age. Rembrandt's only son Titus (1641-1668) was not yet 27 when he was buried in 1668, and his little daughter Titia, Rembrandt's grand-daughter, was born posthumously. Unbroken by the loss of his loved ones or the financial problems that led him into bankruptcy proceedings and forced him to sell his art collection in 1655-1656, Rembrandt was almost as productive in the last decade of his life as he had been in his earliest period in Amsterdam. He was given numerous portrait commissions and painted himself, Hendrickje and Titus in a biblical or mythological context.

The year 1669 is also found on the self-portrait by Rembrandt in London. In the initial design

Rembrandt, 1606-1669 *Self-portrait at the age of 63*, 1669 Canvas, 86 x 70.5 cm London, The National Gallery

(visible under X-radiography) he had depicted himself on that painting holding his palette and brushes – in other words, at work. There, his hair is a little shorter and his face somewhat fuller than in the portrait in The Hague, which must therefore have been made later. This means that it is Rembrandt's very last self-portrait. Although it has sometimes been said that he makes a tired and washed-out impression in this painting, he looks at us with the same piercing eyes and purposeful gaze that are the most characteristic features of the impressive series of self-portraits that Rembrandt produced in the course of his life.

Self-portrait, 1669

Canvas, 64 x 58.2 cm
Inv. 840

On 12 November 1619 a contract was drawn up between Johannes del Rio, dean of the Onze-Lieve Vrouwekerk in Antwerp, and Peter Paul Rubens. The painter undertook to paint 'a panel depicting the story of the Assumption of Our Lady' for a fee of 1,500 guilders. He received the first 1,000 guilders in September 1626, and the remaining 500 guilders followed in March 1627.

The reason for the long delay between the conclusion of the contract and the execution of the commission was that the altar where the painting was to be placed was not completed until 1626. The dimensions involved were gigantic: the altar is 14 metres high and more than 7 metres wide.

Rubens's altarpiece measures 4.9 by 3.25 metres. As a first step towards the making of this monumental composition, Rubens painted the 'modello' discussed here, which may be dated on stylistic grounds in the early 1620s. This preliminary study was intended to give the client an idea of what the composition would look like, so that he could comment on it at an early stage.

Preliminary studies of this kind by Rubens are best characterised as ideas expressed in paint. The rapid execution this implies is also clearly visible in the technique: the paint has been applied off the cuff in rapid movements of the brush. The upward movements give the image a highly dynamic quality. Although Rubens often enlisted assistants to help him with major commissions, it is clear from the high quality of this 'modello' and the altarpiece in the Onze-Lieve-Vrouwekerk that he executed this important commission all by himself.

Peter Paul Rubens, 1577-1640

'Modello' for The assumption of Mary, c.1622-1624

Panel, 87.8 x 59.1 cm

Inv. 926

Jacob van Ruisdael is one of the greatest of Dutch landscape painters. He painted about 700 landscapes of every conceivable kind. The view of Haarlem, the town where he lived until 1657, was one of his favourite subjects. Van Ruisdael depicted it at least fifteen times in the 1670s.

Van Ruisdael painted the city of his birth from the north-west. The characteristic St Bavo Kerk (Church) with its pointed central tower rises high above the city (see p. 67). The accuracy of this scene makes it easy to identify the main buildings: from left to right we see the Bakenesserkerk, the roof of St Janskerk, the 'Klokhuis' (Clockhouse) next to St Bavokerk, the town hall (next to the windmill) and the Nieuwe Kerk on the right. Between dunes and town, long lines of linen are spread out on the fields to be bleached by the sun. Linen weaving and beer brewing were Haarlem's most important industries. The variation between pastures and spinneys gives the painting great depth, which is enhanced by the two sunbeams that illuminate the bleaching fields (a third sunbeam shines on the town). These scattered illuminated patches are characteristic of Van Ruisdael's work. He carefully placed parts of the image in the sunlight, making them gleam even more – some pieces of linen hanging out to dry, for instance, and the sails of a little windmill. Another prominent feature is the impressive cloudy sky, not only one of the painter's trademarks but a highly distinctive feature of the Dutch landscape.

Jacob van Ruisdael, 1628/9-1682

View of Haarlem with bleaching grounds, c.1670-1675

Canvas, 55.5 x 62 cm

Inv. 155

Above the women carving clogs is an inscription on a depot for fire-ladders stating that Pieter Saenredam completed this painting on 20 November 1659 ('P'. Saenredam fecit A°. 1659. 11/20'). That does not mean, however, that this picture is an accurate rendering of the location for that year, since Saenredam worked after a preliminary drawing he had made in 1636.

Pieter Saenredam, 1597-1665
The Mariaplaats with the Mariakerk in Utrecht, 1636
Pen and water colour, 35.2 x 48.7 cm
Utrecht, Gemeentearchief

At the beginning of the seventeenth century little remained of the glory of this old Romanesque church, whose foundations had been laid in 1085. The Iconoclastic Fury of 1566 provided the first assault, and after the 'Alteration' of 1578 the new Protestant city council forbade Catholic worship. From 1619 onwards the church was used by the carpenters' guild, whose members displayed their cupboards and other items of furniture there. The advertising sign above the entrance depicts the interior of the showroom. The weeds sprouting in parts of the eaves are indications of creeping decay.

Saenredam's interiors and façades of Dutch churches exude an air of tranquil serenity. The peacefulness of this scene was the painter's deliberate choice, as the Mariaplaats could be a very busy square: the annual and weekly markets and the fairs were all held here. The closed wooden shutters (possibly concealing stalls) and noticeboard are silent witnesses to these events. The wooden water pump, too, at the left side of the church, was installed in 1617 for the benefit of the market vendors.

Pieter Saenredam, 1597-1665

The Mariaplaats with the Mariakerk in Utrecht, 1659

Panel, 44 x 63 cm
Inv. 974

Michel Sittow portrayed this unknown man against a greenish-blue background, dressed in a brown-coloured gown with a black fur collar and red sleeves. The position of the hands, with the fingers of the left hand seeming to rest on the frame, is derived from Hans Memling (pp. 96-97). The face with its delicate wrinkles is modelled in minute detail using a thin brush, with immense feeling for subtle light effects. A transparent, dark paint has been used to suggest the areas of shade and a light growth of beard, both very delicately rendered. This near-draughtsmanlike technique is the basis for the attribution of this unsigned portrait to Sittow.

Michel Sittow came from Reval (present-day Tallinn) in Estonia, a prosperous Hanseatic town whose official language was Middle Dutch.

He spent his apprenticeship with Memling in Bruges, and went on to become a celebrated international court painter, serving Queen Isabella (1451-1504) of Castile, for instance, from 1492 to 1504. After a period (starting no later than around 1506) in which he worked in his native town, Sittow went to Copenhagen in 1514 to make a portrait of the Danish king. In 1518 he returned to Reval for good.

In spite of his success, few paintings by Sittow have been preserved. Furthermore, since few are dated, the picture we have of his oeuvre is fragmentary. Dendrochronological analysis of the *Portrait of a man* reveals that it probably dates from the first period of Sittow's activity in Reval, between 1506 and 1514. The sitter is therefore most likely a merchant or nobleman of that city.

Michel Sittow, c.1469-1525

Portrait of a man, c.1510

Panel, 34.2 x 24.6 cm
Inv. 832

In this little painting – the smallest one Steen ever made – the painter depicted a very popular theme: a meal of oysters. The young girl holds an oyster that she is sprinkling with a little salt. On the table before her we see a beautifully painted still life of oysters, a Delft blue pitcher next to a glass of wine and a silver tray with salt, a cone bag of pepper and a half-eaten roll. In the background a maid and a servant are preparing more oysters in the kitchen. Oysters are traditionally regarded as aphrodisiacs, placing this scene in an amorous context. The erotic associations of the delicacy are emphasised by the fact that the girl, the only figure depicted prominently, looks straight at the viewer.

She seems to be offering herself as well as the oysters – an interpretation backed up by the presence of the curtained bed behind her.

This painting, which may be dated around 1658-1660, bears a clear resemblance to the finely painted work of Frans van Mieris the Elder (pp. 100-101). The extremely delicate way in which Steen painted the scene in the foreground makes a conspicuous contrast with the background, which is executed in wide brushstrokes. Steen lived in a village near Leiden, where Van Mieris worked, and he seems to have derived not only the style of this painting but also the composition and subject-matter from Van Mieris.

Jan Steen, 1626-1679

*'The oyster-eater', c.*1658-1660

Panel, 20.5 x 14.5 cm (rounded upper edges)
Inv. 818

This highly original portrait of a girl and two servants in a poultry yard, dating from 1660, is one of Jan Steen's best-loved paintings. Here the master displays his talents not only as a portraitist and genre painter, but also as a skilled painter of poultry. Aside from the chickens, pigeons, turkeys, a pheasant and a peacock, the fancy ducks in the foreground also command admiration.

This poultry yard is set against an archway, with a dovecot on the left. The castle in the background has been identified as Lokhorst or Oud-Teilingen near Warmond, north of Leiden, which means that the girl is probably Bernardina Margriet van Raesfelt (1649-1681). In 1660, the 11-year old Bernardina lived at Lokhorst with her foster mother Anna van den Bongard, who derived the usufruct of the castle from her first husband – and first cousin – Cornelis van Mathenesse. The family coats of arms above the archway are those of Cornelis's parents. Since Anna van den Bongard's grandmother had also grown up at Lokhorst, Anna must have regarded it as the family estate. When she commissioned this portrait from Steen, the painter was living close by, in the village of Warmond.

The girl is giving a lamb some milk to drink from a small bowl, while an Italian greyhound is lapping up the spilt drops at her feet. The servant on the right with eggs in his basket and in his apron has brought her the milk. The dwarf in his torn coat who is looking on probably takes care of the poultry. The two servants are both depicted in such a portrait-like fashion that they were probably members of the domestic staff at Lokhorst.

Jan Steen, 1626-1679

Portrait of Bernardina Margriet van Raesfelt (?),
known as 'The poultry yard', 1660

Canvas, 107.4 x 81.4 cm
Inv. 166

Jan Steen often depicted proverbs and sayings. Here he illustrates the saying 'as the old sing, so pipe the young', which appears as a rhyme on the sheet held by the old woman ('Liet / Soo voer gesongen soo / na gepepen ...'). A central image here is 'smoking someone else's pipe', used here as a metaphor for following the wrong example. The painter who allows his son to smoke a pipe is an unambiguous exhortation to parents to set a good example. The boy playing the bagpipes can also be interpreted as an allusion to the subject. The adults are showing the younger generation their bad habits – smoking and drinking. The woman emphasises the latter with her raised glass of wine, the filling of which is the focal point of the picture. The figures have probably gathered to celebrate the baptism of the young child behind the table, depicted between the glass of wine and the sheet with the proverb.

Steen frequently portrayed himself and his family in his genre pieces: in this painting the boys and the girl on the right have been identified as Steen's own children, and the woman as his first wife, Grietje van Goyen (died in 1669). This painting, which may be dated around 1665, is Jan Steen's largest genre piece. The painter depicted this theme in several other paintings, which may be regarded as variants of this one.

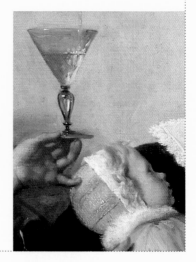

'The way you hear it, is the way you sing it', c.1665

Canvas, 134 x 163 cm

Inv. 742

In this series of five Troost has ironically depicted the course of a typical eighteenth-century social gathering of gentlemen. The title of the five sheets derives from the first letters of the five Latin titles, which are inscribed on the original frames. The first scene shows the party assembled in the salon of a mansion. They fill their pipes, smoke in silence and wait to see what will develop. Some cast furtive glances at the maidservant. By the second scene the atmosphere has relaxed somewhat. A game of tric-trac is in progress and two of the guests are admiring their host's portrait on the wall. In the next scene tempers have become frayed, through a combination of a quasi-scientific debate and the maidservant's deep décolleté.

One of the gentlemen is urinating in a corner of the room. The dinner that follows degenerates in the small hours into an orgy of drinking in which all moderation has been jettisoned. At the end the guests have great difficulty finding their way home.

The series was probably commissioned by Theodoor van Snakenburg (1695-1750), a Leiden lawyer. The scenes have a theatrical air about them, which is hardly surprising as Troost had embarked on a career as an actor at the Amsterdam playhouse around 1720.

Cornelis Troost, 1697-1750

'NELRI' series, 1739-1740
'Nemo loquebatur' (No-one spoke)
All pastel and paintbrush in opaque paint on paper,
*c.*56.5 x 72.5 cm
Inv. 186-190

TOP *'Erat sermo inter fratres' (The brothers conversed)*
BOTTOM *'Loquebantur omnes' (Everyone was talking)*

TOP *'Rumor erat in casa' (There was a commotion in the house)*
BOTTOM *'Ibant qui poterant, qui non potuere cadebant'*
(Those who could walk did; the others fell)

Esaias van de Velde's winter landscapes are in many ways diametrically opposed to winter scenes by his famous contemporary Hendrick Avercamp (see p. 38). While Avercamp gives us – certainly in his early work – panoramas with countless figures in colourful attire, Van de Velde chooses to restrict his subject. No wide vistas but a small section of a waterway near a house. No bright polychrome but a very limited palette that in this case consists only of brown and red. The result is a subdued, tranquil atmosphere. Esaias van de Velde's winter landscapes play an important role in the transition from the anecdotal scenes of the sixteenth century to the pure winter landscapes of painters such as Jacob van Ruisdael (pp. 124-125) and Salomon van Ruysdael (1600/3-1670).

Van de Velde has included only a few figures in this scene: two men with a sledge, two boys playing *kolf,* a boy putting on his skates and a woman with her arms huddled under her apron. As none of the faces is clearly visible – they appear to have their collars up as protection from the freezing cold – they have an air of anonymity about them. Because of this it is not their actions but nature that plays the main part here. The capricious, bare branches that the persistent wind has caused to grow on one side only, the frost on the roofs of the houses, the closed windows and doors and the deserted village all combine to give an impression of the grimness of winter in a Dutch village.

Esaias van de Velde, 1587-1630

Winter landscape, 1624

Panel, 26 x 32 cm
Inv. 673

A group of ships lie at anchor like a choice bouquet. A water tankship lies parallel to the coastline, to its port side a small, flat-bottomed boat with bowsprit rigging. The ship is also flanked by two rowing boats with large fish-baskets. To the right is a large three-master, whose headsail is being lowered. In the right foreground is an official yacht with a richly decorated escutcheon. This escutcheon is surmounted by a shield with three St Andrew's crosses, the arms of Amsterdam, while the right shield displays crossed anchors, the arms of the admiralty of Amsterdam. The most striking element is the cartouche in which a red Dutch lion is depicted with sword and sheaf of arrows against a gold background. Willem van de Velde signed his name on the banderole beneath it. The Dutch flag flies from the mast-heads of most of the ships, the ship at far left being the odd man out – it is an English three-master known as a 'snow'.

Willem van de Velde the Younger probably painted this scene around 1658. At that time he was working in the studio of his father, Willem van de Velde the Elder (c.1611-1693), who was renowned above all for his paintings executed with a pen. Father and son departed for England in 1672; two years later they entered the service of Charles II (1630-1685), and they subsequently served his successor James II (1633-1701). Until 1691 they had their studio at Queen's House, Greenwich. In a large proportion of both their oeuvres the ships are rendered so clearly as to justify the epithet 'portraits'. In eighteenth-century England numerous other artists took the paintings of Willem van de Velde the Younger as their example.

Willem van de Velde the Younger, 1633-1707

Ships on calm water, c.1658?

Canvas, 66.5 x 77.2 cm
Inv. 200

Johannes Vermeer has been extolled down the ages for his virtuoso painting technique, the many finesses of which can be studied in his *View of Delft*. His astonishing control of paint and brush enabled him to achieve any effect he desired, with the accurate rendering of light playing an important part. His work displays everything from a highly precise technique to free, expressive brushstrokes, and from a thick impasto to a thin, almost transparent layer of paint. Sometimes Vermeer would impart structure by mixing the paint with coarsely ground grains of pigment. At right he has suggested the light reflected by the water on the hulls of the moored boats by applying the paint in tiny dots. This 'pointillistic' manner of painting is regarded as one of the most characteristic features of his art.

Vermeer painted this view of his home town of Delft around 1660. We see the city from the south, from the opposite bank of the river Schie. Within the city walls we can make out Schiedam Gate with its clock tower and Rotterdam Gate with its twin towers. Dark clouds overshadow the buildings ranged along the Schiekade. Partly because of this, the eye is led past the bridge between the city gates into the sun-drenched heart of the city, which is dominated by the monumental tower of the Nieuwe Kerk. This gave Vermeer's town view an unprecedented three-dimensionality.

Johannes Vermeer, who started his career as a history painter, acquired especial renown with his masterfully painted scenes depicting one or two figures in an interior. Only two town views by him are known today: this painting and *The little street* in the Rijksmuseum, Amsterdam.

Johannes Vermeer, 1632-1675

View of Delft, c.1660-1661

Canvas, 96.5 x 115.7 cm
Inv. 92

Around 1665 Vermeer painted a number of 'tronies', of which this is undoubtedly the best known and best loved. A 'tronie' is a painted face that is intended not as a portrait, but as a rendering of a particular type or character. Imaginative details of the sitter's apparel are often an important aspect of the picture, as in the case of this girl with her turban and the oversized pearl at her ear. The inventory of Vermeer's property, drawn up three months after his death on 15 December 1675, includes 'two Turkish-style tronies'. This painting may have been one of them. In that case, it was not sold in Vermeer's lifetime.

The exotically clad girl who looks over her left shoulder at us with parted lips is brightly illuminated and set against a dark, indeterminate background. She is painted in an extremely free and expressive style. Tiny dots of paint have been used to add highlights, for instance at the eyes and the corners of the mouth. The pearl is made up of only a few brushstrokes: a brightly lit accent at upper left and the soft reflection of the white collar in the jewel's underside. Since the recent restoration of the *Girl with a pearl earring*, its subtle nuances of light and colour can once again be fully appreciated.

In 1881 the collector A.A. des Tombe purchased this piece at an auction in The Hague for 2 guilders and 30 cents. In 1902 he bequeathed it to the Mauritshuis, along with eleven other paintings.

Girl with a pearl earring, c.1665

Canvas, 44.5 x 39 cm
Inv. 670

Against the background of a landscape identifiable as Flemish from its characteristic buildings, and surrounded by mourning figures, the dead body of Christ is displayed, as it were, to the viewer. At centre, Mary kneels beside her Son, with John supporting her. Her intense participation in the Passion of Christ was seen as an example to be followed by the faithful. At right kneels the bishop who commissioned this painting – probably an altarpiece – in the company of Peter and Paul. His identity remains an unresolved controversy. The curved top of his crook contains a depiction of the Annunciation, the event foreshadowing Christ's incarnation and his later sacrificial death on the cross. Joseph of Arimathea supports the lifeless body, while Nicodemus grasps a fold of his shroud: both are described in St John's gospel. At left are depicted the three Mary's, referred to by Mark and Matthew in their account of this event. At the far left we see Mary Magdalene, identifiable by her jar of ointment. *The lamentation of Christ* is the only work in a Dutch museum by the Brussels painter Rogier van der Weyden, who is regarded, together with Jan van Eyck (*c*.1395-1441), as one of the most important Flemish painters of his day.

Infrared reflectography has revealed a fine – autograph – underdrawing beneath the layers of the paint. Various changes were eventually made relative to this drawing, particularly in the heads and hands. Because the master never dated his paintings, there is a good deal of uncertainty about the chronology of his oeuvre. Dendrochronological investigation of the panel of this work makes it plausible to date the piece to about 1438 or later.

Rogier van der Weyden, *c.*1399-1464

The lamentation of Christ, after 1438

Panel, 80.5 x 129.5 cm
Inv. 264

Nowhere has the potential of copper as a support been exploited to such brilliant effect, perhaps, as in the small paintings by the Utrecht artist Joachim Wtewael. They are executed with immense precision and the finish is as smooth as glass. Because copper is an extremely stable support, they are still in excellent condition after almost four hundred years.

Wtewael has depicted a racy scene from the story of Mars and Venus, as described by Homer (p. 117) and Ovid. Venus, though married to Vulcan, is regularly unfaithful to him with Mars. When Vulcan finds out he forges a fine bronze net and spreads it over Venus's bed. Venus and Mars become entangled in the net while making love, at which the cuckolded husband displays them to the assembled gods. Contrary to his expectations, however, the gods are not enraged but amused. Mercury, who pulls aside the curtain in this scene, even confesses that he would be happy to change places with Mars.

Wtewael lived in Italy from 1586 to 1596, where he became acquainted with painting on copper and with Mannerism. This picture shows the full range of his marvellous painting technique. The elaborate detail, subtle use of colour and superb Mannerist poses make this work a feast for the eyes. The artists' biographer Karel van Mander (1548-1606) saw the painting and described it in his *Schilder-Boeck* (1604) as 'a most excellent small piece of copper … brimming with enjoyable minute details / and so sharp'.

Joachim Wtewael, 1566-1638

Venus and Mars surprised by Vulcan, 1601

Copper, 20.8 x 15.7 cm

Inv. 223

CONTRIBUTIONS
Ben Broos
introduction and pp. 40-45, 62-63, 66-67, 88-89, 110-117, 120-121
Quentin Buvelot
introduction pp. 27-29 and pp. 58-61, 98-101, 130-131, 134-135
Peter van der Ploeg
pp. 32-37, 46-49, 52-55, 68-69, 78-79, 82-87, 92-95, 102-103, 106-109, 118-119, 122-123, 126-127, 136-143, 150-151
Guus Sluiter
pp. 64-65, 70-75, 80-81, 124-125
Ariane van Suchtelen
pp. 38-39, 50-51, 56-57, 76-77, 90-91, 96-97, 104-105, 128-129, 132-133, 144-149

TRANSLATION
Beverley Jackson, Amsterdam

EDITING
Quentin Buvelot

DESIGN
DeLeeuwOntwerper(s), The Hague

PRINTING
C. Chevalier bv, Hendrik-Ido-Ambacht

ISBN 90-76764-03-4